Best Wishes
John Sewer.

Brian Hardie

Summer of Success

Summer of Success

The Triumph of Essex County
Cricket Club in 1979

David Lemmon

Pelham Books
LONDON

For VAL
and for the suffering
wives and girl friends of
Essex County Cricket Club

First published in Great Britain by
PELHAM BOOKS LTD
44 Bedford Square,
London WC1B 3DU
1980

ISBN 0 7207 1255 6

Composition by Cambrian Typesetters
and printed and bound in Great Britain by
Billing & Sons Ltd, London, Guildford and Worcester

Contents

Acknowledgement

The short extract from the article by Roger Edson and Pat Hodges is reproduced by kind permission of *Wisden Cricket Monthly*.

Introduction

At 5.30 on the afternoon of Tuesday, 21st August, 1979, Brian Hardie stroked Jim Yardley's third delivery of the season for the run which gave Essex a remarkable victory by seven wickets over Northamptonshire.

Having disposed of Northamptonshire for 224 on the Saturday and finished the day at 82 for 1, they looked set for the twenty points which would give them the first championship in their one-hundred-and-three-year history.

On the Monday they had faltered badly and were out for under two hundred, so failing to gain two batting bonus points. Then Stuart Turner had launched his heart and soul into the attack to bring his haul of wickets in the match to ten and Northants were out just before twelve on the last morning and Essex needed 229 to win.

This was a time for wisdom and maturity, and Denness and Hardie had abundance in both. The score was 113 before Mike Denness fell to Williams. Ken McEwan hit a massive six then fell to Peter Willey. There must be no panic now. Fletcher, all elegance and resolution, joined Brian Hardie who now looked impregnable. They added 78 before Fletcher edged Larkins to Yardley at slip, but the skipper left knowing that there were wickets and time in hand for the nineteen runs that were still needed.

Keith Pont played a couple of handsome shots and then allowed Hardie his valiant hundred and, deservedly, the winning hit.

Joyful, but apprehensive, the Essex players clustered round the radio to listen to cricket scores which were still half an hour away. Then the news came that Worcestershire had failed to win at Derby, and Essex knew that they were county champions for the first time in their history.

Unbeknown to all others Peter Edwards, whose energy and enthusiasm as secretary-manager had burnished the cause of Essex cricket across the country, had stacked some bottles of champagne in the boot of his car in anticipation of this moment. And as the bubbles sparkled and the handshakes and embraces took place, there was amid the elation a tiredness and a sense of flatness almost as if the weight of a century-old history of fruitless endeavour was slipping from weary shoulders.

For those who sipped champagne in the pavilion at Northampton that night, for Graham Gooch doing his bowling impersonations at Headingley, for Jackie, Barbara, Enid, Stanley, Roger, Pat, Bill, George, David and the rest of the supporters, for Peter Edwards and his staff, for Tom Pearce, for Doug Insole and the committee, it had all begun four months before.

In truth, it had begun 103 years before and these were the actors in the finale of a great drama of courage, perseverance and the giving of joy.

CHAPTER 1

Years of Endeavour

There had, of course, been Essex county sides before 1876. Thomas Lord's first cricket ground, the present site of Dorset Square, was opened in 1787 with a match between Middlesex and Essex. Eleven years previously Essex had played Kent at Tilbury Fort, but Essex County Cricket Club was formed at a public meeting held at the Shire Hall, Chelmsford, in January 1876.

The first Chairman of the Essex County Cricket Club was James Round, M.P. for Colchester, and it was he who led the side.

Most of Essex's early cricket was played at Brentwood, and it is, perhaps, ironical that by the year of triumph Brentwood had ceased to be a county ground. The isolated nature of the Brentwood ground in the nineteenth century, a characteristic it retained until after the Second World War, led to the County looking for a home which would attract greater support. They chose Leyton, a rapidly expanding London suburb, and matches were played there for the first time in 1885. It is sad that none were to be played there in the memorable summer ninety-four years later.

In 1894 the County gained first-class status though they did not enter the county championship until the following year.

There were two bowling performances in that year of 1895 which stand as county records to this day. H. Pickett took all ten wickets for 32 against Leicestershire at Leyton and the great Walter Mead took 17 for 119 in the match against Hampshire at Southampton.

Until a few years ago Walter Mead's son still lived in Billeri-
cay, and on his Sunday walks in Lake Meadows he enjoyed the
local cricket, dispensing wisdom and kindness to all he met.

In that first year in the county championship Essex finished
equal with Somerset in eighth place. The two counties were to
be linked as the Cinderellas of first-class cricket until the
memorable events 84 years later.

These were what have since been described as golden years of
cricket. It was the age of F.S. Jackson, A.C. MacLaren, C.B. Fry,
'Ranji', 'Plum' Warner, Tom Hayward, George Hirst, Gilbert
Jessop and W.G. himself. But Essex had her own legendary
figures. Apart from Walter Mead there was the fearsome Charles
Jesse Kortright, deemed by many to be the fastest bowler of all
time, and Percy Perrin, one of the greatest of amateur batsmen
never to play for England.

In 1898, at the height of the golden age, Essex finished third
in the county championship. Little was it realised then that this
was to be the pinnacle of their achievement for the next eighty
years.

The early part of the century saw Essex struggle for both
success and support. There were moments of brightness. In
1904 Percy Perrin hit 343 not out against Derbyshire at
Chesterfield. This remains a county record and with triple
centuries practically extinct, it is a record likely to remain for
ever. Perrin, a strong but kindly man, served Essex and cricket
with distinction, and was a Test selector until the outbreak of
war in 1939.

In 1901, a young man straight from Felsted School had made
his debut for Essex against Yorkshire. He had bagged a 'pair',
bowled by George Hirst in both innings. His name was J.W.H.T.
Douglas. He was a man of immense courage and application.

He did not establish himself in the Essex side as a dour batsman and a fine bowler of above medium pace until 1908. By
that time he had won the Amateur Middleweight Boxing
Championship of Great Britain and was the Olympic Champion.

In 1911, Douglas was appointed captain of Essex, a position

he was to hold for 17 years. He was shocked and hurt when he was relieved of the captaincy at the end of 1928 and he never played for Essex again.

Two years later he was killed at sea. He was returning to England on the passenger ship *Oberon* which sank after colliding with another ship, the *Arcturus*. Douglas was drowned in trying to save the life of his father. He was 48 years old.

He captained England in triumph, he took over from the sick 'Plum' Warner in 1911-12 when England beat Australia 4–1, and in adversity. His defensive batting earned him the nickname of Johnny Won't Hit To-day from the Australians.

He was a man of tenacity and resolution and he carried Essex cricket on his broad shoulders for nearly two decades. Cricket history has done him scant justice and even his obituary in Wisden was grudging in its praise.

The last years of Douglas's captaincy saw the advent of players who were to serve Essex with skill and wholehearted endeavour until the outbreak of war. Outstanding among these players who made their debuts in the 1920s were Jack O'Connor, Stan Nichols, Lawrence Eastman and Jim Cutmore.

Jack O'Connor was coaching and playing golf until his death in 1977 and Jim Cutmore played in a Keith Fletcher benefit game at Chelmsford in 1973 at the age of 75. As in his younger days, he refused to give his wicket away.

Morris Stanley Nichols was a true all-rounder, a medium pace bowler and a fine batsman, who did the 'double' eight times and played 14 times for England. A neat and accomplished man, he packed his dancing shoes with his cricket kit when on tour, for he was complete in the social graces.

Nichols's most memorable achievement was in the game against Yorkshire at Huddersfield in 1935. Yorkshire had not been beaten for a year and they were destined to be champion county in 1935, but Nichols's performance will never be forgotten. Yorkshire were bowled out for 31 and 99. Nichols took 11 for 54. Essex scored 334. Nichols made 146. It was one of the few bright Essex lights of the thirties.

Essex had an abundance of fine cricketers and colourful characters, but rarely could the talents and the temperaments fuse into an all conquering combination. The policy of shared captaincy could not have helped.

The thirties is littered with players and counties making their record scores against Essex.

In 1932, Sutcliffe and Holmes made their world record opening stand of 555 for Yorkshire against Essex at Leyton. The same year at Chesterfield, G.M. Lee and T.S. Worthington put on 212 for the sixth Derbyshire wicket against Essex, a county record. Two years later, Ashdown and Frank Woolley joined in a Kent record second wicket stand of 352 against Essex at Brentwood.

This match, in fact, was the reintroduction of county cricket to Brentwood. Kent scored 623 on the opening day. They declared at 803 for 4. Ashdown scored 332, Woolley 172 and Ames, dropped when 30, 202 not out. Ashdown's score and Kent's total are county records to this day.

O'Connor and Pope hit hundreds for Essex, but Kent won by an innings and 192 runs.

Kent's record breakers had not finished with Essex. At Colchester in 1938, Arthur Fagg became the first batsman in cricket history to hit two double centuries in a match and he and Sunnucks were engaged in a Kent record opening stand of 283 in the second innings. Revenge was to be a long time in coming.

In 1939, Essex were fourth in the county championship, the highest position they had occupied since 1898, but their hopes of further glory were shattered by the war.

When first-class cricket resumed in 1946 age and the war had taken its toll of Essex cricket.

Kenneth Farnes, a natural fast bowler of world class, Lawrence Eastman and Claude Ashton, a member of a distinguished family which has stamped its name indelibly on Essex cricket, lost their lives in the war; others had passed from the scene.

The job of rebuilding was given to Tom Pearce who was made captain, a position which he had previously shared. Tom Pearce first played for Essex in 1929. He was to become a Test selector, chairman and finally president of Essex County Cricket Club. He could have wished for no greater reward after fifty years of unstinting dedication to Essex cricket than the glories of the summer of 1979.

At 74 years of age, Tom Pearce was as active as ever in the Essex cause in 1979, speaking a few words in aid of a Stuart Turner benefit collection or simply exuding kindness to all he met, always with his wife by his side.

The first season after the war was notable for the arrival of 'Dickie' Dodds, a quick-scoring opening batsman, and a young all-rounder named Trevor Bailey. The cousins Peter and Ray Smith were still in action as was that fine batsman Sonny Avery.

County cricket lives because of cricketers like Ray Smith. He had the potential to become a quick bowler of Test quality, but the war years, when he was the leading light of the British Empire XI, and the fact that he bowled more overs than almost any other bowler in the country in the years immediately after the war, dampened the fire. He is part of the history on which the summer of success is founded.

So, too, is his more famous cousin, T.P.B. Smith. Peter Smith played for Essex from 1929 to 1951 and during that time took 1611 wickets, more than any other Essex bowler. He played for England, not merely as a leg-break bowler, but as an all-rounder. After the war he dropped down the order and in 1947 found himself going in at number eleven against Derbyshire at Chesterfield. He and Frank Vigar added a county record of 218 for the last wicket. Peter Smith scored 163 which is the highest score ever hit by a number eleven batsman.

Peter Smith's record was rather overshadowed the following season when Essex played the Australian touring team at Southchurch Park, Southend. This was the great Australian side of 1948, Don Bradman's last tour of England. The Australians scored 721 on the first day, the highest total ever recorded in a single day's play in first-class cricket. As a consolation Essex were the first county to bowl the Australians out in one day!

Such hammerings haunted the history of Essex. A year later, at Fenner's, John Dewes and Hubert Doggart were unbeaten in a second wicket stand of 429, which was not only a Cambridge University record for that wicket, but also an English record and only 26 short of the world record. The Cambridge captain was Doug Insole and making his debut for Essex that day was a sixteen-year-old wicket-keeper named Brian Taylor.

In 1950, Doug Insole joined Tom Pearce in the leadership of Essex. This did not mark a return to the unhappy policy of the 1930s. Tom Pearce was now 45 and a Test selector. The decision to appoint Insole as joint captain was a rightful grooming of the heir apparent. The following season Trevor Bailey became assistant secretary to the club and in 1955 he succeeded Mr. H.G. Clark as secretary.

Thus, by the mid 1950s, the four men whose patient efforts were slowly to transform the club were established in key positions in Essex cricket; Tom Pearce, chairman; Doug Insole, captain; Trevor Bailey, secretary; Brian Taylor, wicket-keeper and fitness fanatic.

The Essex side of the early fifties had been champions of brighter cricket, but, though they may have scored runs more quickly than other sides, they conceded them with equal alacrity. Now, by the end of the decade, a formidable side capable of challenging anyone was beginning to take shape.

Bailey had become an established Test cricketer and one of the cricket legends of his time. History will stamp him as 'Barnacle Bill', but there were times when he did more than hang on. In an aggressive mood he had some superb leg-side shots, and there were times in those early post war years when he looked as if he would be England's answer to a prayer for a fast bowler. In the end he settled for fast medium and batting of resolution, but in all his guises he was a man of character, humour and benevolence.

His enthusiasm still graces the game and his undisguised joy at the Essex triumphs of 1979 gave the commentary box a vibrant humanity.

Trevor Bailey was first tutored by Denys Wilcox, a fine bat and an excellent pre-war skipper of the County. Wilcox was headmaster of Alleyn Court School, Westcliff-on-Sea, a preparatory school now most capably run by his son, John Wilcox, who has also played for Essex. Bailey moved to Dulwich, Cambridge and the Royal Marines, and came to the fore in those entertaining matches at Lord's at the end of the war.

Younger than Bailey by three years, Doug Insole is one of those men who is blessed with all round qualities as both sportsman and administrator. On and off the field he led Essex into a new era.

In 1979, twenty years after the event, Doug Insole was still haunted by a game between Essex and Kent at Blackheath.

He had taken Essex there as championship leaders, clearly ahead of their nearest rivals. On the Saturday Essex made 371, but with Bailey and Ralph unable to bowl, Kent reached 560 for 6 before they declared. Colin Cowdrey hit 250 which was the highest score he ever made in first-class cricket in England. The match was drawn thanks to a splendid rearguard century by Trevor Bailey, but the Essex dream was over. In the next five weeks until the middle of July, they failed to pick up a point and they finished ninth in the table.

Insole recalled this match at a reception two days after the Prudential World Cup Final in 1979. Essex should have been playing Kent at Tunbridge Wells at the time, but the match was rained off. We had been enquiring for news of the match and it was suggested to Insole that the Essex lead in the championship was certain to bring them the title. He shook his head mournfully and reminded us of Blackheath, 1959, and what followed.

Insole's dream was not to be realised during his own period of captaincy, but surely no one has made a greater contribution to Essex success. A man of the utmost integrity, with a quick intelligence and a quiet charm, Doug Insole has been a bastion of English and world cricket for a generation. His management of the 1978-9 England side in Australia won the highest possible praise, and he has brought his assessment of people and his sensitivity to their needs to the cause of Essex cricket over a period of nearly thirty years. It was the deepest sadness that the year of the Essex triumph should be marred for him by personal tragedy.

The duties of Test selector absorbing more and more of his time, Doug Insole relinquished the captaincy at the end of 1960. He was succeeded, automatically, by Trevor Bailey.

The early sixties were not an easy time for Essex either on, or, financially, off the field. There was a need for reassessment of the playing strength and a drastic reappraisal of how the club was run on a business basis. Bailey had struggled manfully to combine the jobs of captain and secretary, but the task was becoming too heavy even for his broad shoulders, and in 1966 Major 'Topper' Brown became secretary.

Cricket historians will probably assess Bailey's period of captaincy as something of a disappointment, an Eden, the best already behind him, following a Churchill. This would do him scant justice. In 1962, he gave the first opportunity to an elegant teenager, Keith Fletcher, and within the next five years he brought Acfield, East, Turner and Lever to the county staff. Moreover, when Bailey toured the West Indies with the Cavaliers in 1964-5, he discovered a young Barbadian all-rounder named Keith Boyce. Others, like the exciting Peter Spicer, shone for a brief moment, but with players like Barker, Edmeades and Hobbs already established, the end of Bailey's term of office saw Essex with the nucleus of a fine side.

Bailey's reign ended in 1966. He was succeeded by Brian Taylor. His task was not an enviable one. Disagreement over benefits and over who was to succeed Bailey caused Barry Knight, who had forced his way into the England side as an all-rounder, to sever his connections with the county and to join Leicestershire. Other retirements followed.

A sub-committee, of which the present chairman 'Tiny' Waterman and Doug Insole were members, investigated the club's financial plight and applied ruthless economies. Within a short time Taylor was to be asked to operate with a playing staff of thirteen. Second-eleven cricket almost disappeared and administrative costs were cut back. There was a surge of fund-raising activities. Jack Insole instigated a system of redemption of Green Shield stamps. Money was borrowed from the Warwickshire Supporters' Association, to whom Essex owe undying gratitude, and a new pavilion was built at Chelmsford, now established as the County headquarters. Inevitably, this meant the gradual disappearance of county cricket in Brentwood, Clacton and Romford, and, more recently, at Leyton.

The new pavilion was the first step in a series of projects aimed at making Chelmsford worthy of becoming a county ground. In the 1960s the press accommodation at Chelmsford was a tent which, seemingly, always faced the wind. The lavatories on the popular side of the ground, buckets and tents, were the greatest incentive to membership and the right to use the pavilion ever devised by a county. Application, dedication and effort by a band of people has changed all this and these barbarisms are now part of history. Chelmsford County Cricket Ground is now a place of brick-built arbours, executive suites and an indoor cricket school; and there is promise of more to come.

Taylor had no illusions about the task that faced him when he took over the captaincy in 1967. There have been better cricketers than Brian Taylor, but very few have accomplished as much in the game or served it as well. At one time he had been seen as a possible England wicket-keeper. He was voted 'Young Cricketer of the Year' in 1956, and he had toured South Africa with the M.C.C. in 1956-7 as Godfrey Evans's deputy, but Murray, Parks, Smith and Knott were Evans's successors and honours never came 'Tonker's' way again until, briefly, he was a Test selector.

He led Essex for seven years and he led them with firm

discipline. He took a bunch of talented, promising, but untried young men and taught them to be professional cricketers. The first sign of unrest at debatable decisions on or off the field was quelled with the stentorian tones of 'Right lads, leave this to me.' And they did.

He insisted on standards in dress, blazer and tie, and in fitness. He frogmarched professional cricket onto a level comparable with other professional sports as he demanded a course of pre-season physical training which at first amused, then frightened other counties into imitation. Essex became the most exciting fielding side in the country and, as runners between the wickets, they had no equals. As dedicated to Essex cricket as he is to his mother, his wife and family, he continues as committee man, captain of the second eleven and inspiration to young players. Some may have disagreed with Brian Taylor, none ever disobeyed him.

His first achievement was to repair the morale of a wounded side. This accomplished, he pointed them towards success in the limited-over competitions which seemed particularly suited to their talents, aggressive batting, superb fielding, tight bowling. They had shown little aptitude for the Gillette Cup in its early days, but they gained instant success in the John Player League. They were third in the first year of the League, 1969; fourth in 1970, and, cruelly, second in 1971.

In 1971, Essex finished their Sunday-league fixtures on 29 August with a victory over Warwickshire which meant that they led the table by four points. The following Sunday Worecestershire beat Warwickshire at Dudley inside 18 overs and so finished level on points with Essex, but took the title with a faster run rate, .003.

The same season Essex were engaged in an emotional Gillette Cup quarter final with Lancashire at Chelmsford. They lost by 12 runs and Lancashire went on to win the cup.

In 1972, having dismissed Middlesex at Westcliff for 41 and won by 8 wickets in the second round, Essex again found themselves in the quarter finals. This time they met Kent at

Leyton. They bowled Kent out for 137. Keith Fletcher had been taken ill and was replaced at the last minute by Ken Wallace, one of the finest of club cricketers, whose first-class record compares favourably with many more regular players. Wallace and Edmeades put on 55 for the first wicket and Essex seemed assured of victory. They were all out for 127, and the bogey of Kent was to stay with them for the best part of another decade.

It certainly haunted them again the following season. In the quarter finals of the Benson and Hedges Cup Essex easily defeated the favourites, Leicestershire, and they went to Canterbury for the semi-final with a certain amount of confidence. They restricted Kent to 169 for 9 in their 55 overs and went to tea at 60 for 1 with Bruce Francis and Keith Fletcher in command. In the pavilion at Canterbury that day Kent members were asking what it felt like for Essex to be in their first final. We were never able to tell them. Essex were all out for 123 with 11 of their 55 overs unused.

The ultimate success was to be denied Brian Taylor and, in 1974, now 42 years old, he handed over the captaincy to Keith Fletcher who had been his vice captain and fellow team selector for several seasons. Ronnie Cox had also replaced Major Brown as secretary, but the policy remained unaltered — economic stability and cricket for the enjoyment of players and spectators.

With much of his time spent playing for England, Fletcher's first year of captaincy was not an easy one, and much of the time Robin Hobbs led the side. Fletcher had grown up with most of the side that he was now asked to lead and he was confronted with the problem of stamping his own brand of personal authority on a group of lively personalities. With patience, firmness and calm, he achieved his aim, and Essex again contended for honours.

In 1977, Essex went to Scarborough for the penultimate match in the John Player League as leaders in the competition. They lost in the last over to the blows of Bairstow and Johnson. The following week they beat Worcestershire at Chelmsford, but Leicestershire also won. Both counties finished on 52 points, but Leicestershire took the title with more victories than Essex.

In the dressing room, after the defeat at Scarborough, Stuart Turner had wept openly. He had bowled with his usual accuracy until Bairstow had savaged him in his last over to make the Yorkshire victory possible. The most wholehearted and dedicated of professional cricketers, Turner blamed himself entirely for the Essex defeat. Fletcher is not one given to easy praise or flippant compliment. He walked over to Turner and said, 'Stuart, but for you we would never have reached this position. You have done more than anyone to get us here.' There was no-one in the Essex camp who would have disagreed with the captain's judgement of the worth of this splendid all-rounder. Team spirit is more than a journalist's phrase in Essex cricket.

Still they were left with the nagging feeling that they were born to be second, and nothing that happened in 1978 detracted from this feeling. In the Schweppes County Championship they were beaten only once, by Surrey at The Oval, but they chased Kent all the way and were denied the title only in the closing week of the season. They finished 9 points behind the Champions and their second place was the highest in the 102 year history of the club. They also reached the semi-final of the Gillette Cup for the first time ever. Somerset made 287 for 6 in their 60 overs at Taunton. Essex needed three to win off the last ball. Neil Smith was narrowly run out in going for the third run. Essex were out for 287. They lost because they had lost more wickets than Somerset. It was the match of the season. It was wonderful cricket. Everybody loved the spirit with which Essex played their cricket, but they still had not won anything.

Then came 1979 — the summer of success.

CHAPTER 2

The Cast

The cast assembled for the dramatic year of 1979 was one of trusted and proven ability. It was the finest blend of youth and maturity.

The leading actor was a man of complete dedication to the game of which he possessed an astute knowledge. He drove others no harder than he was prepared to drive himself. Shy, self-effacing, Keith Fletcher possesses none of the qualities associated with extrovert captains like Tony Greig, but his cricket brain is second to none, a fact indeed which was recognised by Greig himself when he insisted that Fletcher be in the England party on what was to be the last tour before the Packer affair. Greig leaned heavily upon Fletcher, conferring with him as with a lieutenant.

By 1979, Fletcher had been an Essex professional for seventeen years, but in a distinguished career he had received few of the accolades that were his due. One of the few class batsmen of his generation, he had received an unhappy baptism in Test cricket which some never forgot. He was brought into the England side for the fourth Test against Australia at Headingley in 1968. He fielded at first slip and missed a couple of difficult chances. The Yorkshire crowd believed that Sharpe should have been in the side and Fletcher received no sympathy from them. He made 0 and 23 not out.

He played 52 times for England between 1968 and 1977. He scored just under 3000 runs in Test cricket at an average of over 40 and he hit seven Test centuries. In the 1970s only five batsmen scored more runs in first-class cricket. Yet in spite of his splendid Test record, his consistency in first-class cricket and his having the best cricket brain in England, his lack of flamboyancy and an image cultivated by the media left him a maligned and most unjustly criticised man.

Some supporters, fretting for success, blamed him for the lack of it. Rather than praise him for bringing Essex the closest that they had ever been to glory, many blamed him for the ultimate failure.

The brickbats that Fletcher had received were few as compared to those received by Mike Denness. Succeeding Colin Cowdrey as Kent skipper, Denness had led the side with distinction. Under his captaincy they had won the John Player League three times, the Benson and Hedges Cup twice and the Gillette Cup once. He had become captain of England and, at first, was successful. Then he had had the misfortune to lead England when Thomson and Lillee were at their height. His batsmen were neither used to, nor capable of dealing with, such pace. England were trounced and Denness was replaced as captain. After the 1976 season he left Kent and came to Essex on a three-year contract.

Cricket News suggested that his only contribution to Essex cricket was to keep a young, home-grown player out of the side. This was as unfair as it was shortsighted. Denness brought to Essex not only stable and experienced batting, but the sweet smell of success. At last there was somebody in the Essex side who had actually won something, who had been at Lord's receiving a trophy in front of a huge crowd, and this mattered. With Denness, Essex cricket gained a new dimension.

The move from Kent, a county which takes itself rather seriously, to Essex, the county with the reputation of being the greatest comedians in cricket, could not have been entirely easy for Denness. He fitted admirably.

'I was greeted with remarks like "Here's our guest player. Do you think you'll last three years?" Then one day I bought a new suit and arrived at the game feeling good and thinking I looked pretty smart. But after Ray, Stuart, J.K. and the rest of the lads had finished with me, I was looking in the mirror at the end of the day, saying "Well, I thought it looked all right, but . . ." Within days of being here I felt completely at home. The whole team always stays behind for a drink after the game and this is very important because we are together socially and we are together as a team.'

Denness's contribution has been incalculable. He brought the belief that victory was possible and he brought a soberness which took away none of the fun, only channelled it in the right direction, at the right time.

Ray East is a joker, a man who controls his passionate concern for the game and for his county by his clowning. He is not the Fool who wanted to play Hamlet, he is Hamlet who plays the Fool to conceal the agony. A man with an undying belief in the dignity, the rights and the equality of human beings, Ray East's dedication to the Essex cause has never flagged since his debut in 1963 when he was 18. The love and esteem in which he is held by the Essex crowd was reflected in the benefit he received in 1978. He responded by having a bumper season.

A keen student of the game, he allies brilliant fielding and batting of well-above-average ability to the left-arm spin bowling which brought him a hat-trick in a Test trial. It is England's loss that he was never selected for the Test side. He would have brought a sense of fun to the Test arena which would have been like a breath of fresh air in the spiteful cauldron of the mid-seventies. Viewers all over the world would have seen those beseeching appeals when Ray implores the umpire as Al Jolson used to implore his 'Mammy'. The world would have been better for the sight.

East's fellow spinner is David Acfield. Cambridge Blue, Olympic fencer, *cognoscente* of birds, western films and country and western music, Acfield brought a quiet and unassuming intelligence to the Essex side. He has had to grow philosophical about the role of the spinner in modern cricket.

Often omitted from a side in search of extra seam, the

spinner has been reduced to the position of one who bowls while the seamer is resting. The decline of the spinner's role is as marked in the England side as in any county side.

Acfield uncomplainingly accepted this position which meant his virtual exclusion from the one-day game and spasmodic appearances in the championship side. His talent and determination were reflected in the way in which he grasped the opportunities that were given to him.

Another who had to grasp limited opportunities was Keith Pont. A young man of undoubted talent whom former teammate Bob Cooke sees as an England player, Pont had been impetuous in his desire to play shots. This impetuosity was not a failing which would be cured by the over limitation in county cricket which consistently relegates those batting at number six or seven to a ten-over slog.

As a seam bowler he had opened the bowling for the English Schools; as a batsman he was one of the hardest hitters in the game with a splendid record of sixes in the John Player League. He had first played for Essex in 1970 at the age of 17, but he had had to wait another six years before being capped. He had not been the luckiest of players. He once scored a century in the county championship, only to be left out of the side for the next match. His moment of glory would come in 1979.

1979 was Stuart Turner's benefit year, and none would begrudge him such a year. An aggressive cricketer, passionately committed, Stuart Turner forced his way into county cricket by sheer application and by pushing himself almost beyond the limits of his ability. Few men have given more of themselves to cricket than Stuart Turner; many lesser men have taken more from it. If the spirit of Essex cricket is encapsulated in one man, that man is Stuart Turner. He is the true all-rounder. He bats, bowls and fields with zest. His concern is for the side and for the game.

He dreads inactivity and, as his attractive wife and lovely children will tell you, the approach of the cricket season means the cleaning out of cupboards and a general sense of physical urgency.

Stuart Turner was capped in 1970, the same year as John Kenneth Lever, the best left-arm quick bowler in England. John Lever is a young man of modesty, intelligence and charm. He has been one of the best and one of the unluckiest bowlers of his generation. He has been an almost constant twelfth man for England, sometimes being passed over for bowlers who could not compare with him in either form or fitness.

He has accepted all uncomplainingly and his dedication to fitness and team spirit ultimately gave Essex a winning dimension. He is a bowler whose ability has been underrated by many of those who write upon the game; never underrated by those who pay to watch it.

For two years he was voted the 'Players' Player of the Year', a testimony to the worth with which he is considered by his fellow professionals. A superb fielder, a consistent wicket taker, he was cruelly and stupidly omitted from the England fourteen for the Prudential World Cup in 1979. J.K. threw off his bitter disappointment to answer the selectors with the eloquence of 53 wickets in a month.

John Lever's partner as opening bowler was Norbert Phillip. In 1977, Keith Boyce had been forced to retire from first-class cricket because of injury. Boyce was, and is, much loved in Essex cricket circles. His explosive contributions as batsman, bowler and fielder have made him among the most popular and most exciting cricketers in the country. When he finally gained Test recognition his success surprised only those who had seen little of him with Essex. When his enforced retirement was announced at Southend during a John Player League match in 1977, his benefit year, there was a sense of sadness and of a void in the world of Essex cricket.

How would Essex replace him? Whoever was brought in to replace Boyce held an unenviable task. The name of Richard Hadlee had been mentioned, but he joined Notts. There were rumours that a former Lancashire bowler would be coaxed from retirement. In the end Essex signed 'Nobby' Phillip, an all-rounder from Dominica, unknown outside the West Indies.

'Nobby' had none of Boyce's instant extrovert appeal. He came to Essex as a twenty-nine-year-old of unknown quality. In the March and April of 1978 he won three Test caps for the West Indies when the Packer players walked out. He opened the bowling for the West Indies in their tour of India, 1978-9. He bowled his heart out on wickets which gave him no encouragement and finished the series in second place in the bowling averages with 19 wickets. With the return of the Packer players he was left out of the West Indies side.

In his first year with Essex he scored 645 runs and took 71 wickets. In an amazing display of hitting at Gloucester he had thrilled the cricket world with a maiden hundred that had given Essex a sensational victory, but it was as a bowler that he was most valued.

Mike Denness believes that it was the arrival of Norbert Phillip that turned Essex into a championship winning side. 'Fast bowlers have always gone in pairs — Larwood and Voce; Lillee and Thomson; Lindwall and Miller. In his last couple of seasons Boycie was struggling because the poor lad was never really fit. With "Nobby" at the other end John became a better bowler, for there was now no respite for the batsman. And "Nobby" is quick. A few people don't realise quite how quick he is.'

No bowlers succeed without good fielding and wicket-keeping. The Essex fielding, as with their running between the wickets, was the best in the country. Their wicket-keeper had few equals.

There is the feeling that because a player has been released by a county he is not really good enough and whoever signs him is getting second best. One needs only to look at the careers of Younis, Barry Wood, Derek Taylor, 'Pasty' Harris, Keith Stevenson, Mike Taylor and many others who were, at one time, 'not re-engaged' to realise that this is nonsense. It should not be forgotten that Bob Willis was allowed to leave Surrey without being capped. The same fate awaited Neil Smith. He had been groomed as successor to Jimmy Binks, but was jettisoned by Yorkshire after eight matches. One remembers a meeting with a Yorkshire league umpire in Kent three years ago. His comment was succinct. 'From Essex? You've got Neil Smith there. Ay, we let the wrong chap go.'

In 1979, there were none in Essex who would disagree with this statement. In the daily grind of first-class cricket, only Bob Taylor of Derbyshire and Derek Taylor of Somerset could equal him in consistent application.

Neil Smith was brought to Essex to succeed Brian Taylor. His weakness was symptomatic of the whole team — he could never believe how good he was. In 1979 moments of greatness were to come to him in no small measure and they were richly deserved by this shy, happy, sensitive man whose mere presence gave confidence and joy.

At the same time that Smith had been signed Essex had signed a Scotsman named Brian Hardie. Hardie was from a sporting family. His father and brother were cricketers and the family also has an alliance with Stenhousemuir Football Club. 'Lager' had proved his pedigree with his success in Scotland's representative matches. For Essex he made an instant impact as a dour opening bat.

The success as an opener had faltered, but Hardie had learned about professional cricket. He drilled himself into becoming the best bat and pad fielder in the country, taking a series of amazing catches at 'Boot Hill'.

In the batting order he had dropped to number five, a move that was beneficial to both player and team. One remembers a conversation with Mike Brearley at Westcliff in 1972. Middlesex had narrowly escaped defeat and Brearley was most impressed with the Essex side. His one reservation was: 'If only they had something at number five.' Brian Hardie provided that something. Playing within his capabilities, he had found aggression and power. The concentration and application and sound defence remained, but the stodginess was gone. His five years as a professional had been dedicated to the 'getting of wisdom'. Now he was to reap his reward.

As opener he had been succeeded by Graham Gooch. Those like Bill Morris, Harold Faragher and Trevor Bailey who saw Gooch play at the age of sixteen considered him to be the most exciting prospect seen in Essex cricket since the war. An innocent young man of immense talent, he had been thrust into the England team in the last days of Mike Denness's reign and the first days of Tony Greig's. His baptism had been fearsome. A period of uncertainty had followed. Keith Fletcher then made the decision that Gooch should open the innings in an effort to give him time to play an innings and develop his ability. That was the beginning of the 1978 season. It was a wise decision. Graham was recalled to the England team. He prospered against Pakistan and New Zealand — the New Zealanders considered him the only batsman, apart from Boycott, who was capable of taking a hundred off their bowling. In Australia he learned and matured.

He began 1979 as the most exciting batsman in English cricket. His one problem remained, to turn himself from a scintillating 70 run man into an eight century a season man. He had an abundance of ability and power. Now he needed sustained concentration to make him probably the outstanding batsman of his generation.

Coming in at number three was Ken McEwan, a South African, who, bewilderingly, had been released by Sussex in 1973 and joined Essex the next season. There are those who believe that Ken McEwan rivals Viv Richards as the best batsman in the world. Any who saw McEwan's destruction of Underwood at Tunbridge Wells in 1976 can understand why this claim is made. A charming, quiet, shy, nervous man, McEwan's languid style presumes a confidence which, initially, his batting lacks. His timing is perfection, his range of strokes unparalleled. His batting is the excitement of great art. In one over of the Tunbridge Wells innings mentioned above, he square cut, pulled and straight drove Underwood for four off three successive deliveries. No fielder could move to any one of the shots. Here was batting in the grand manner.

When McEwan is out a sigh of regret goes round the ground from friend and foe alike. The same sigh used to accompany the dismissal of Denis Compton. For, as with Compton, when McEwan is gone, a beauty and excitement go with him. It was apparent to all that if Essex were ever to win anything, much would depend on Ken McEwan.

These twelve players were the assembled cast which would provide the platform for the success of Essex. Denness and Phillip had joined within the last two seasons, but the rest had been together for the best part of five years. At the end of 1979 when people were trying to analyse the reason for the success of Essex the general cry was that everybody in the side was able to make a contribution of some sort. This was true, but it had been true for some years without Essex winning anything. Why should 1979 be any different?

John Lever would point immediately to a crucial factor. 'For the first time we could trust what we had in reserve. We knew that if anyone was out of the side through injury or playing in a Test, we had lads whom we could rely on when they were brought in.'

Alan Lilley had proved this point with a hundred on his first-class debut against Notts in the last match of the 1978 season. He was too sensible a young man to believe that he would be able to repeat this in every game that he played, but he was totally dedicated to cricket and ever willing to learn.

Lilley's arrival in first-class cricket was a testimony to his own hard work and the foresight of some sound cricket judges. He had represented Essex Schools with modest success — his top score being only 34 — but he had been highly valued by Stuart Turner, who had coached him, and by the Ilford club, who gave him every opportunity.

With Stuart's encouragement he went for a trial to Lord's for a place on the M.C.C. ground staff. He was accepted and worked with great intensity. Within two years Len Muncer had contacted Keith Fletcher and said quite simply, 'You must sign this boy.'

At the beginning of 1979 it was decided to play Alan Lilley in all the one day competitions which would mean Mike Denness standing down, but Mike saw that Lilley, an investment for the future, must be given match practice.

Pressing Lilley hard for a first team place was Mike McEvoy who had taken his opportunities in the championship side well and had had the feel of first-class fifties. A product of Roger Bayes's Colchester Royal Grammar School side, McEvoy is an intelligent, warm and likeable young man who is dedicated to the hard job of learning to be a professional cricketer. He is a superb slip fielder and he gives a confidence in Essex cricket for years to come.

Waiting in the wings, too, were Reuben Herbert, a prolific scorer in the Truman League with Orsett, but of great interest, too, for his off-spin bowling, and Gary Sainsbury who looked like a carbon copy of John Lever.

Wisely cajoled by Brian Taylor, these young men provided the backbone of reserve strength, the strength in depth, which is a necessary part of the equipment for any side which pretends to honours.

The cast was assembled. 'With such troops as those we'll be lords of the game.'

CHAPTER 3

Backstage

Behind the scenes there had been significant changes in production when the curtain on the 1979 season was raised. A chartered secretary from Leicester had been appointed secretary-general manager. His name was Peter J. Edwards, A.C.I.S. He was an Essex fanatic, hailing from Southend, and his impact was dynamic.

On the business side he drove Essex to success. He wanted everyone to live and breathe Essex cricket, and few could refuse him. He tightened organisation and increased efficiency, and this flowed onto the field. Like Fletcher, he demanded nothing more than he was prepared to do himself, and like Fletcher he was surrounded by a superb team.

Ronnie Cox, nearing retirement, became fund raising secretary. Ronnie is a cultured and civilised man who exudes goodness wherever he goes, and it was right that he should be part of any Essex success.

The same was certainly true of Jeanette Carman whose attractiveness was a vital part of the Essex scene. As assistant secretary (membership) Jeanette had the unenviable task of answering members' queries and placating them when they were irate. She managed to stay in firm control of any situation with her vivacity and irresistible charm.

Jeanette was not the only lady to make a marked contribution to the summer of success. She had gained an assistant in Jackie Stanley, a quietly efficient young lady whose job it was to monitor the score cards, look after visiting Access and Benson and Hedges ladies and to become the voice on the telephone which gave callers the latest score. This was one of Peter Edwards's innovations. Having been a frustrated Essex supporter living in Leicester, he knew only too well the difficulties and agonies of trying to find out how things were going with the team. During match days at Chelmsford, the line to the cricket school became a number which one could ring to obtain the latest recorded message giving one the score. Jackie's was the voice on the recorded message and she it was who kept the score up to date.

Valerie Moth, Peter's secretary, had been with the club for over four years before he arrived. Her efficiency and easy control were just what was needed to complement Peter's zest.

Without these people the club could never have functioned. The whole organisation depended upon them and upon the energy of nineteen-year-old Mick Glover who acted as Peter Edwards's assistant. It depended upon the accountancy skills of Ken Illingworth who spent three days a week at the club seeing that the books were in order. Like Peter Edwards, Ken is a chartered secretary and a vital cog in a well run business machine.

None of the administrative staff could have even begun their work without the faithful service of Dorothy Geer who has kept the County headquarters clean and tidy for several years and to whom success means as much as it does to anyone else on the staff.

Much of the success of any county cricket club is due to the efforts of a committee who give of their time freely and whose dedication and enthusiasm, particularly in times of adversity, are the life-blood of the club. In this respect Essex have been no exception and have been well served over the years by many who wish only to give to the game that they love and to their own county.

'Tiny' Waterman, the present chairman, is a former treasurer of the club and has worked unceasingly for nearly 40 years (he made his debut for Essex in 1937) for the good of Essex cricket. He is a quiet and unassuming man, but, as a chairman, firm and decisive. His approach to Essex cricket typifies the positive approach to all affairs, on and off the field, that the County has striven to encourage.

The post of treasurer is now filled by Peter Keith. Peter was once a familiar sight at Essex home games as he toured the ground selling books and souvenirs in the cause of Essex cricket. For years he has been the motivator of the Essex supporters' club whose role is now being taken over by the Essex County Cricket Club Development Association. The reason for this shift in emphasis is that it is no longer possible for an amateur organisation to market all those products which are now being offered in order to raise money for the future of Essex County Cricket Club, a realistic attitude which partly accounts for the solvency of Essex.

The Development Association is chaired by committee man 'Jerry' Jerman, who leads the professional team of director Preston Keeling, secretary Anthea Yandell and assistant Mike Chapman.

L.C.S. 'Jerry' Jerman played one game for Essex in 1951, against Surrey at Southend. He opened the bowling and did not take a wicket. Surrey made 423 for 9 declared and Essex were 314 for 9 against Bedser, Laker and Lock when 'Jerry' joined Trevor Bailey. Ken Preston had been out on the last ball of a Laker over and Bailey farmed the bowling so that it was several overs before 'Jerry' faced his first ball in first-class cricket. He hit it for six. He has maintained the same pugnacious attitude in his unstinting work on the Essex committee.

Like 'Jerry' Jerman many other members of the committee are former club cricketers, and like him many have a great urge to win. One thinks, for example, of John Jarvis with his concern for youth and his business acumen attending meetings and functions practically every night of the week in the service of cricket in general, and Essex in particular.

John Jarvis's work for the National Cricket Association and the Essex Cricket Association is shared by Mike Chapman. Mike himself is not one of the world's great cricketers, but the time, the encouragement and the money from his own pocket that he has given on behalf of youngsters are impossible to record. He is not alone in Essex in this unselfishness. David Bradford, David Holland, Gwynne Harries have all given so much, not least on behalf of the young; and Reg Hilliard, the mastermind behind the Young Essex side and a leading enthusiast for the establishment of the cricket school at Chelmsford, has stamped his name indelibly on the history of Essex cricket.

In the service of youth none has done more than Harold Faragher. Harold played for Essex as an amateur in the early fifties and met with some success. Before the war he had played for Lancashire second eleven. His teaching commitments kept him from full time cricket, but he combined both his talents in founding the Ilford Cricket School at Beehive Lane. Here with the magisterial Bill Morris, himself a former Essex player, who instils the ethics of cricket as well as the skills into his charges, he has nursed many eager boys towards a higher standard of cricket. Among the Essex players who were coached initially at the Ilford school are Lever, Gooch, Pont and Lilley, but there are few in the present side who have not sought the advice and help of Harold and Bill at one time or another.

The County headquarters at Chelmsford now has its own cricket school where Bob Richards is chief coach. Bob succeeded Graham Saville after the first month of the 1979 season when Graham moved to his position as regional coach with the National Cricket Association. Graham's busyness about the grounds was symbolic of the Essex attitude and Bob is a worthy successor for he is one of those busy wicket-keepers of club cricket. The Savilles remain firmly entrenched at Essex for Graham's brother Tony has charge of the dressing rooms.

Tony is one of those seen busily engaged on match days; another is chief steward Peter O'Connell. When a club is successful every other match becomes a big event and the job of the stewards becomes more and more taxing. Peter O'Connell headed a team that was used to big crowds and was ready for more success.

The work of others goes on before the match day. Head groundsman Eddie Neath and his assistant Nicky King had toiled for the best part of three years to give Essex wickets which would produce good batting while never making the bowler's task a ludicrous one.

The work of the groundsmen is noted and commented upon by all who watch cricket; the work of Frank Harris is taken for granted, noted only when something goes wrong which, with Frank in charge, it never does. Frank Harris is the ground maintenance foreman of Essex County Cricket Club. Like fourteen other counties Essex play their home games at more than one ground. It is Frank's task to supervise the movement of seating and all that is necessary to stage a game of first-class cricket. The mind finds it difficult to imagine what is involved in the transference of all the paraphernalia associated with a cricket match from Chelmsford to Southend to Colchester to Ilford and back to Chelmsford. Frank Harris can conceive the work involved and the operation runs so smoothly that few of us ever realise anything out of the ordinary has taken place.

Ray Cole is another whose work may go unnoticed by the general public, but whose very absence from the scene of action can cause a wave of uncertainty to pass through the dressing room. Ray Cole is a physiotherapist who serves Essex, Colchester United and many less sporting patients. The pressures of modern sport are intense and Ray Cole must eliminate aches and pains, real and imaginary. Physically and physchologically, he is a vital member of the team.

So, too, in to-day's game of limited overs and fines for slow over rates, are the scorer and his helpers. John Burgin, retired policeman, controls the scoreboard at Essex home matches with a verve, gaiety and speed which reflect the team itself. The man who feeds him the information is scorer Clem Driver.

Clem Driver had moved into the position of scorer in succession to Jack Bartlam. A successful businessman who had masterminded Keith Fletcher's benefit and helped with the benefits of others, Clem had retired and spent his retirement in the pursuit of his love, cricket. He knows and loves the game at all levels. Completely unflappable, possessed of a dry wit and a quick mind, Clem Driver had been a calm and balanced part of the Essex cricket scene for several years. It was right and proper that he should be part of any success.

These then were some of the people assembled backstage. They were to be responsible for the fluency of production.

The cast fretted eagerly in the wings, 'like greyhounds panting in the slips'.

The audience took their seats.

CHAPTER 4

The Audience

The inhabitants of a county impose their personality upon the cricket team that they support. It is well known that Yorkshiremen will endure no frivolity; with Glamorgan cricket there is a sense of exuberant suffering; in Sussex it is a regal, careless, seaside abandon.

The county of Essex is not the largest in England, but it encompasses much. There is Essex-London; Newham, Barking, Dagenham with their heavy industry and cockney inheritance. There is Colchester, a beautiful town divided between ancient history and the modern army. To the north of Colchester is the peaceful Suffolk border country. To the west and south is the busy rural town of Saffron Walden, defiantly retaining old traditions and architecture in the face of a commuter housing explosion, and the quiet charm of Thaxted. The south Essex border is the Thames with the Londoner's seaside at Southend and the more imposing Leigh and Westcliff. There are the new concrete creations of Basildon and Harlow, soulless monuments to a new order, dwelt in by people struggling to identify with town and county. And in the middle there is the county town of Chelmsford, valiantly fighting to retain character and charm amid the ravages of a one way traffic system and the junction of main roads.

There are the inevitable rivalries which divide a county; north of Chelmsford versus the south; parochial interests; from country areas feelings of neglect by central authority.

From these diverse places and characters has been fashioned a county personality. It is a personality which combines the cultural elegance of a county rich in history with the brisk demands of modern commerce: it fuses rural wisdom with urban wit. The county cricket team must reflect this personality.

The support for any county is part ephemeral, part loyal. The loyal core is what matters for it is they who will pay the wages, even in the darkest days. The Essex audience is more faithful than most; the loyalty has been earned by a team who have never stood apart from those who come to watch them.

Like true men of the soil the Essex supporters had accepted the disappointments with a weathered philosophy, but within them all throbbed the repeated question 'Will we win something this year? Next year?' The end of the 1978 season had left most of them feeling that the great opportunity had been missed, that perhaps they would never come so close to honour again. But adherence to a cause, to a team, is founded on the undying optimism that El Dorado is round the next corner. You may never state this belief in public, but you hold it in your heart. Some, like Frank Wilmott, had held it in their hearts for over fifty years: others, like Kevin Montgomery with his meticulous scoring and records, had nursed the belief for only a short while in their young lives.

Bill Bradley had occupied his place in the front row of the Chelmsford pavilion for as long as one could remember. A former schoolmaster, his life had been given to Essex cricket, first in the organisation of junior county sides, now in his permanent adherence to the fortunes of the seniors. Not optimistic by nature, he was conditioned to Essex failures by the years of their falling at the last hurdle. His loyalty remained unquestionable though he sighed and cursed at the follies of youth on the stage set before him. He sat firm in his seat in the stalls, hoping that one day. . . So, too, did his friend Laurie Weston who still administered the affairs of Essex schools' sides along with George Talbot, angry that Leyton no longer counted as a home ground for the county. On the field before them these two recognised some who had passed through their hands.

Completely different in character is Enid. She bubbles with

optimism and never misses a match, nor a ball that is bowled if she can help it. She had holidayed in Australia in support of Mike Denness's team. Her grandchild was christened wrapped in a shawl that had once kept a baby David Acfield warm, a link as necessary in folklore to Enid as the something old, new, borrowed and blue to the bride. Always excited with news, taking over the supporters' shop at a minute's notice, probing eagerly at what would come next, Enid occupies a unique place in Essex cricket. Her absence would leave a void.

Business commitments mean that Stanley is able to see only parts of games. Dickens would have loved this jovial and alert man who rushes from his work in Coggeshall to all parts of the country in pursuit of Essex. He is a bringer of joy. An abject performance will draw from him the gentle remonstrance that 'they were rather silly on Sunday.'

Pat and Roger, and one speaks of them as of a straw hatted double act, are keen students of the game. Club cricketers of good standard, they bring a passionate sense of commitment to their observation of cricket. They read widely on the game, listen avidly, arrange their family holidays after carefully studying the season's fixture list and feel an emotional allegiance to the County side, some of whom they knew in less illustrious days.

What, too, could success mean for Leslie Newnham who for years had kept the Essex statistics in good order?

More detached, but no less committed, is Norman Cuff. A man of rare wit and good fun, Norman had been the butt of the jokes of his friends in the Cricket Society for many years. Members of Middlesex, Kent and Surrey, they looked at Norman's Essex tie with indulgent humour. Like many another man Norman Cuff had to wait his time patiently.

So, too, did the faithful Queenie, the Gooch family, Ena and Robert Acfield, Roy Pawsey, John Vincent and Peter Roberts whose energies had brought about the formation of an Essex Cricket Society, David of Chelmsford, Cathy, the Baileys and their dogs.

Patience was to be rewarded. In retirement the Reverend Philip Wright, former rector of Roxwell, collector of farming mementos, fervent follower of Essex cricket and lover of its countryside, dispenser of good humour in the Chelmsford pavilion, was to gain his reward for a lifetime's devotion which was second only to his devotion for his maker.

There was to be a reward, too, for George who, in his work for the Eastern National Bus Company, had often come closer to the team than most and had shared their disappointments and joys.

These were some of the audience which gathered for the summer of 1979.

CHAPTER 5

The Curtain Rises

'April,' according to Mr. Eliot, 'is the cruellest month,' and as the weather which inevitably greets the English cricketer at the beginning of the season would be more appropriate to Siberia than to Lord's or Cambridge, it is not difficult to agree with him. Nevertheless, a few people gathered at Lord's to see M.C.C. entertain Kent, the County Champions, and rather more went to Fenner's to see Cambridge University play Essex.

There can be few places better than Cambridge in which to begin a cricket season. The air of Cambridge is good. Perfumed by centuries of great minds, it enters one's heart and, as when one is in Sandwich or Wells, one feels, momentarily at least, that all one's dreams are possible.

It was an ideal place for Essex to begin a season. It was reunion time. Norbert Phillip was still in the West Indies, but Ken McEwan was back after his winter, not in South Africa, but playing grade cricket in Perth. Graham Gooch, looking older and wiser, and John Lever were back from Australia. Lever had to take a little teasing for the Australian cricket magazine's description of him as 'big, beefy and blond'. There were many handshakes and warm greetings for friends not met since September, but, above all, there was a sense of fitness and eagerness.

There were nets set up just outside the boundary and Chris Gladwin, Mike McEvoy and Reuben Herbert practised under the guidance of Brian Taylor and Graham Saville. Mike Denness, whose wealth of experience was not being pitted against the undergraduates, was dressed in a white and red Essex track suit.

He punctuated spells in the nets with laps of the field and short sprints. From time to time he was joined by Ray East or any member of the side not at that time directly engaged in the game. There was an air of physical urgency and meaningful activity.

Brian Taylor was concerned with both sides as he had taken over as coach to the University side who showed much promise in this game and could boast one or two young men of undoubted ability.

Cambridge won the toss and batted on the Saturday. Lever and Pont opened the attack and before the day was through Turner, East, Gooch and Acfield all bowled a few overs. Surprisingly, John Lever was the only one who could not find his real line or length. Mills and Mubarak put on 29 for the first wicket before Gooch took the first of his four catches. In no time the University had slumped to 49 for 5 and would have been in a worse position had not Greig, who ended as top scorer, been missed first ball off Turner. They closed at 197 and with Graham Gooch and Alan Lilley scoring 62 in the hour and a half that remained, Essex had made a highly satisfactory start to the season.

Dreams of century starts to the season evaporated quickly on Monday morning when Lilley ran himself out and Gooch edged the excitingly promising Surridge to the wicket-keeper. McEwan and Fletcher batted with good sense and McEwan promised an exciting innings until he gave wicket-keeper Cotterill his second catch, this time off the bowling of Popplewell who later in the year was to make his debut for Somerset. The honour of the first Essex fifty went to Keith Fletcher. In retrospect it was right and proper that he should be the first to pass the fifty mark for Essex in 1979 though few of us at Fenner's that day could realise that we were witnessing the beginning of an historical year in first-class cricket.

Ray East had lost none of his sparkle in the winter. He bemused some unknowing Cambridge supporters in the pavilion with a running commentary in which he described the innings of Fletcher and McEwan as 'thoroughly boring'. 'McEwan has just hit that through the covers for another boring four.' The dismissals of McEwan, Pont and Fletcher brought the commentary to an abrupt end with 'Blimey, I'm in next.'

Brian Hardie and Stuart Turner played with heart warming, early season assurance. Derek Pringle, playing against his own county, had bowled Pont with a shooter, but he could not reproduce this against Turner who hit him straight for the first six of the season, a splendid beginning to a memorable benefit year.

Just before four o'clock with Essex 253 for 5 torrents of rain fell and play ended for the day. It did not begin again until after two on the last day when Hardie reached his 50 and Essex passed 300. Cambridge lost Mubarak and Holliday for 3, but Mills and Dewes prevented further disaster and the game, not surprisingly, was drawn.

It had been a most satisfactory beginning to the season, not in that any sensational victory had been achieved, but as Graham Gooch had put it 'Everybody had a chance to do something. Everyone got a few runs and all the bowlers had a bowl.' It was an ideal loosener, but there were more difficult tasks ahead.

It was at this time that John Lever put to the team a new idea which, while in itself not seemingly revolutionary, was to have a great effect on the events of the following months in that it brought the team even closer together.

Half of the county cricket season sees a county side playing away from home and living in hotels. Like most counties Essex had the policy of room sharing; John Lever had always shared with Boycie, then with Norbert Phillip; Ray East had roomed always with David Acfield. John's idea was that they should change room-mates for every match. His reasons were simple. East and Acfield, for example, were both spinners who could endure a day's cricket in which they saw themselves as stopgap bowlers, bowling only to give the seamers a rest. After such a day they would be tempted to brood on their discontent

together in a hotel room, to take their troubles to bed with
them. Similarly, the seamers would react when they stood idle
on a spinner's wicket. Professional cricketers, like children at
school, would always rather be in the thick of the action.

John Lever's idea, which he had brought from his experiences
with the England side, was to break up partnerships which
could become introvert and self pitying and to integrate the
side to such an extent that each man became fully aware of the
other's needs and responsibilities. The suggestion was greeted
with some hostility, and rightly, for it was difficult to see how a
side could have a better morale or a greater respect for each
other's talents than Essex, but the Essex side is wise in cricket
and in the way of the world, and it was decided to try the
scheme. The decision was not regretted.

There was one more game to be played before the end of
April, against Warwickshire at Edgbaston on the opening
Sunday of the John Player League programme. Gooch opened
well and Pont and Hardie supplied the later fireworks, but 174
for 8 was a moderate total. It was too much for Warwickshire,
however. The home side began confidently, but Ray East again
proved that accurate slow bowling is as effective in limited-over
cricket as it is in the three-day game. In his eight overs he took the
first three Warwickshire wickets and exposed the frailty of what
was to come. Lever and Pont ran through the tail and Essex won
by 15 runs, quite a substantial margin in John Player League.

The country was now gripped by miserable weather and the
general election. Both of these events tended to obscure the fact
that the two counties who had contended for the Schweppes
County Champtionship in 1978 were contesting in the opening
match of the county championship in 1979.

It was bitterly cold at Chelmsford on Wednesday 2 May and
though the sun shone spasmodically, the wind dominated. No
play was possible before 12.15 and when Fletcher won the toss
Denness and Gooch began the season sweatered against the
cold. Only 49 overs were possible before squalls of rain brought
play to an early close. At 128 for 3, Fletcher 41 not out, Hardie

15 not out, Essex could be well satisfied with their start against the champions.

The contentment ended abruptly on Thursday morning, polling day, when both Fletcher and Hardie were caught at slip off Hills within three overs for the addition of one run. Underwood had moved ominously into the attack and Kent threatened to conquer. Fletcher's instructions to Pont and Turner were quite simply to get after the bowling. It was an order which was welcomed by two players whose natural instincts were to attack. In 50 minutes of exhilarating cricket, which was never anything other than batsmanship, they added 75 runs and Essex passed the 200.

As Pont and Turner attacked so Kent wilted. At the start the ball had lifted nastily on the damp pitch; now it was rarely allowed to bounce. Both batsmen moved quickly down the pitch and Shepherd, in particular, received savage treatment though it was he who broke the stand when Pont failed to get to the pitch for once and edged to Woolmer in the gully. The score book registers him as scoring 33, but Pont's knock was worth many a higher innings scored on brighter and less taxing days. It certainly helped to speed his father's recovery from a bout of sickness.

Norbert Phillip, who must have shuddered at the change of climate he was experiencing, was in the Essex side for the first time in the season and now joined Stuart Turner. The pair were together for just over an hour. At first Phillip was content to watch Turner's vigorous swing of the bat, but soon he found his own timing as if restless to be a mere onlooker. Within minutes the West Indian's bat was winding in a great arc and the ball was soaring to all parts of the field. They added exactly 100. Jarvis had bowled 10 overs for 32 runs, now he was hit for 45 in 6 overs. Johnson's three overs cost 38 runs. Four times the ball was sent hurtling out of the ground and the reserve strength was employed in recovery.

Eight sixes were hit in the innings and the hapless Johnson was plundered for five of them. Phillip and Turner scored at the rate of more than five an over. The fun ended a few minutes before lunch when Turner did not follow through completely and lofted Underwood to Hills. He had scored 102, the fourth century of his career, in ten minutes under two hours. Only Procter, Kapil Dev and Ken McEwan were to hit faster centuries during the summer. He hit 5 sixes and 9 fours. It was an innings to relish and remember. It was a magnificent launching to his benefit year and it sparked an Essex flame which was to burn brightly for the rest of the season.

Fletcher declared at lunch with the Essex score at 305 for 7 made in 90 overs. In the last 38 overs they had scored 176 runs for the loss of Pont and Turner.

The Kent innings was of a much different character. By the end of the day they were 150 for 2. The runs had been scored on a wicket now dry from the wind and had taken 65 overs. The Essex bowling had been tight and the batsmen could not afford the heroics which Essex had demonstrated. Unbeaten for 64 on Thursday evening when Mr. Callaghan was Prime Minister, Charles Rowe remained unbeaten after Kent had used the 110 overs that were their due. Rowe batted for six hours and when the innings was closed Mrs. Thatcher was the leader of the country. Essex led by 55 runs.

The Essex second innings caused mild flutters in the heart as batsmen rushed like lemmings to destruction. At 26 for 8, Phillip and Lever restored sanity and the game was drawn which had looked likely from the start because of the weather. The significant fact was that Essex had taken 6 points to Kent's 5.

Early season fixtures now demanded that the championship be put on one side for four days as counties concentrated on two one-day competitions. Essex had had no game on the first Saturday of the Benson and Hedges tournament and their programme opened with a difficult tie at Northampton. The game was important for, with Combined Universities whom all counties were expected to beat as one of the teams in Group C, whoever won at Northampton was in a good position to qualify for the quarter-finals of the competition.

Again the day was bitterly cold and Jim Watts adopted what was to become common practice in one-day cricket in the season when, on winning the toss, he asked Essex to bat. It was difficult to agree with his decision as, on a slow pitch with bowlers' fingers numbing, Gooch and Lilley started briskly. They had put on 67 when Lilley attempted to hook a ball from Willey that kept low and was leg before wicket. McEwan tried to force too soon and was caught in the covers. Gooch played an innings of calm and power and was finally dismissed in the forty-seventh over when a century seemed to be his for the taking. Fletcher helped Gooch in a stand of 96 in 23 overs and the captain was not out until the final over of the innings which had produced a highly satisfactory 230 for 5.

East was absent from the Essex side with a nagging thigh injury and the opening attack failed to make a disturbance in the calm with which Cook and Larkins began the Northants innings. It was David Acfield who struck the crucial blows for Essex. The openers had put on 85 in 24 overs when Acfield threatened to slow the scoring rate. Cook moved down the wicket to try to hit Acfield high to the boundary only to be caught by Gooch at deep mid-off. Two overs later Larkins went the same way. Willey was out of touch, but Allan Lamb immediately showed the class that makes him one of the most exciting batsmen in English cricket. Jim Yardley gave noble support with some fierce off-side shots until he missed a straight one from Norbert Phillip. Watts was out before another run was scored, but at 197 for 5 with four overs left, the game was still poised. Lamb's splendid innings came to an end when, having already hit two sixes, he aimed to hit Lever for a third and was caught on the leg-on boundary by Keith Pont. Northants then needed 14 runs to win off sixteen balls, but the heart of the batting was gone and Essex won by three runs.

In the frenzy of the closing overs Keith Fletcher had handled his side with admirable calm, a quality recognised by Bill Edrich who gave him the gold award.

If the game at Northampton had illuminated all those qualities which can make limited-over cricket so exciting, the game at Chelmsford the following day reflected the reverse. The meagre Derbyshire batting could muster only 114 and with Gooch again in regal form Essex trotted to an eight-wicket victory. The only memories left by the game were a sparkling catch by Turner, shortly after Tom Pearce had said a few kind words in favour of his benefit year, the grotesque shot with which David Steele sacrificed his wicket, and the nagging feeling that Alan Lilley had to work on a weakness outside the off stump. The seven days that followed were to be the least successful that Essex were to enjoy for the next three months.

The match against Middlesex at Lord's ended at 3.30 on the Thursday afternoon when the rain which was to prevent any play on the final day began to fall. What had preceded the rain was not the most enterprising cricket of the season. On a good wicket Middlesex had batted laboriously. Only Edmonds and Emburey showed any aggression and their efforts were cut short when Brearley declared with five balls of the hundred overs still remaining. Presumably the England captain's declaration was aimed at denying Essex the possibility of another bowling point. The declaration was accepted as a compliment that Essex were a team feared in high places.

The Essex innings was a little more exciting with Ray East, who came in as night watchman though still troubled by injury, once more displaying that he was a batsman worthy of a place higher in the order than number nine. 'He'd be opening for Glamorgan,' as one non-Welshman remarked.

Ken McEwan, though not at his best, was top scorer with 66. He had one remarkable escape when, just before lunch on Thursday, he edged a ball from Selvey to Gould. The wicket-keeper threw the ball in the air in triumphant celebration, but he failed to catch it as it came down.

In the first two rounds of championship matches only Somerset and Hampshire had managed wins. The four points gained at Lord's brought the Essex total to ten and put them in fourth place — sixteen points behind the leaders, Somerset. As their two wins in the John Player League put them joint top of the embryo table and they had won their one Benson and Hedges game, there was a feeling of satisfaction. Then came the week-end of 12 and 13 May.

Surrey were something of a bogey team for Essex. The one Essex defeat in the Schweppes County Championship in 1978 had been at The Oval, a defeat which, arguably, had cost Essex the title, and Essex had never beaten Surrey in the Benson and Hedges tournament. That run was not to be ended.

Surrey began doggedly. Butcher was caught behind off Turner with the score at 22, and Clinton occupied 28 overs in scoring 18. Then Knight and Howarth added 105 in 20 overs and Surrey reached 207 for 6 which did not seem too formidable a total to chase. There was, however, in the Essex team a belief that 'We're no good at chasing runs', and it took much of 1979 to eradicate this superstition.

18 for 2 with Gooch and McEwan back in the pavilion did nothing to increase confidence and just as Lilley and Fletcher appeared to be pulling the game round Sylvester Clarke bowled Lilley and Hardie with successive deliveries. Fletcher, again in splendid form, and Pont now tilted the match in Essex's favour as they attacked the bowling and saw Essex past 150. At 156 Hugh Wilson surprised Pont with extra pace and bowled him. Stuart Turner went first ball and suddenly Essex were beaten by 7 runs in a fine game of cricket.

The same could not be said of the game at Southampton the following day when Essex were on television for the first time in the season. It was not a performance to captivate an armchair audience. Essex were quite dreadful. Their batting was anonymous mediocrity, and Greenidge and Turner treated the bowling as if it were in the same category.

Mid-May is, however, no time for reflection. The weather had been generally cold and miserable and wet. The football season had dragged on endlessly and as yet the cricket season itself was without shape. Hampshire, Somerset, Kent, Middlesex, Yorkshire and Gloucestershire had all flattered, but some at least would deceive. There were no post-mortems for Essex. They journeyed to Derbyshire for their first hotel living of the season.

Just as Middlesex had gained an undoubted advantage from batting first in the drawn game at Lord's, so Essex were grateful that Fletcher won the toss at Chesterfield though their start was not auspicious.

Mike Denness was caught at cover from a rather ambitious shot and Ken McEwan holed out on the leg side off a long hop. Graham Gooch, eleven in the first 25 overs, had begun circumspectly and now he was joined by Keith Fletcher who was missed at third slip, a difficult chance, off Hendrick when 5.

Gooch took 164 minutes to reach his first 50 which he did by pulling Miller over mid-wicket for 6. By mid-afternoon Essex were in complete control. Gooch launched a violent attack on the Derbyshire bowling. He drove Miller belligerently onto the roof of the pavilion. Russell was pulled viciously over mid-wicket and then driven massively over long on. His second 50 took only 66 minutes. He and Fletcher added 100 in 196 minutes, but when the stand had reached 148 and Gooch's score was 109, the opener gave himself room to slash a ball from Barnett through the covers, missed and provided the young leg-spinner with his first wicket in first-class cricket.

The outstanding contribution of the day, however, was that of Keith Fletcher who hit his first hundred for Essex for two years. If one wishes to probe for the reasons for Essex success in 1979, one must understand immediately that the form of Keith Fletcher was one of the greatest reasons for their success. It is worth noting in contrast, for example, that in the season which preceded the tour of Mike Denness's team to Australia, 1974, Fletcher had only once reached 50 and Essex had finished twelfth in the table.

Since the arrival of limited-over cricket, Fletcher, ever looking for improvisation founded on perfect technique, had evolved a shot wherein he retreated to leg and slashed the ball through the off-side field. Invented as a counter to defensive bowling, it was at times productive and at other times could result in grotesque dismissal, as at Southampton on the Sunday before the game at Chesterfield. Against Derbyshire on that Wednesday afternoon, however, it was just one of a whole range of splendid shots that brought him a six and 18 fours in his 140 not out. His innings was to win him the *Sunday Telegraph*– Victoria Wine Company Cricketer of the Week award, so following his team-mate Stuart Turner in collecting a crate of champagne.

The Derbyshire bowlers were handicapped late in the day when, after a forty minute stoppage for a shower, they bowled with a wet ball, but earlier in the day, with conditions in their favour, they had failed to grasp their opportunity. Essex grabbed their chance immediately. Facing a total of 335 from which they had extracted only one bowling bonus point, Derbyshire lost New Zealander John Wright bowled by Lever for 0, and they closed the day at 4 for 1. Rain was in the air — again.

On the Thursday rain fell and only two hours' play was possible. The pitch was damp from the rain that had fallen during the night. The before-lunch session was divided by a thirty-minute shower, but nothing could quench the appetite of the Essex bowlers. With the ball lifting and moving, 'Nobby' Phillip and Stuart Turner destroyed Derbyshire. All out for 63 in under 29 overs — Phillip 5 for 23, Turner 3 for 12, Lever 2 for 20 and eight catches of high and eager quality. John Lever was swinging the ball massively in the Derbyshire second innings when rain saved the home side from further torment.

There was to be no respite on the last day. The pitch was cruel and John Lever exploited it to the full. Derbyshire were 44 for 7 at one time, but in the end they just passed the hundred. Essex held eight more catches, Neil Smith uncharacteristically missed a stumping off David Acfield and Lever had 6 for 52. Essex won by an innings and 171 runs, and by 20 points to 1. On Friday evening they were joint top of the Schweppes County Championship table with Somerset.

The first win of the season feels good whoever you play for. Nobody took the fact that Essex were joint top of the table after three matches very seriously but when we woke up on Saturday morning the sun was shining, Essex were playing Combined Universities at Chelmsford and it really seemed as if the cricket season had begun.

Combined Universities were not expected to pose any problems to a county side though they had given Northants a bit of a fright. The selection of their side, by telephone calls between the two captains, was hampered by injuries and examinations. It was not the strongest side that could have been put in the field and one feels that there is a need for a reassessment of the way in which this Combined Universities team is selected and brought together for what is a highly competitive and lucrative competition. Ian Greig won the toss and asked Essex to bat. In the light of what happened in the next two hours, it is interesting to learn that had he won the toss, Fletcher would have asked the Universities to bat.

By lunch 36 overs had been bowled. On the last ball before lunch Gooch was out. He hit Cooper hard and high to deep mid-on where Mubarak took a fine catch. Gooch had scored 133. The Essex score was 223. Let us say immediately that the bowling was not of the highest quality and that the Combined Universities side lacked a sense of unity and purpose, but the Universities' attack did include Aamer Hameed who had been a member of the Pakistan touring side to England in 1978, Derek Pringle who had played for Essex in 1978 and, if he can bring serious application to his cricket at every level, could become one of their key players in the future, New Zealander John Ross, a young man of considerable talent, and Ian Greig who later in the season was to play for Sussex.

The batting before lunch on Saturday, 19 May, 1979, at Chelmsford was a spectacle of disciplined aggression. Gooch built his innings and Alan Lilley took the opportunity to bide his time, play his shots and occupy the crease as long as possible. With the ball kept up to the bat Gooch was quickly onto the front foot, driving long and hard. When the ball was dropped short he pivoted swiftly and pulled it mightily to the leg side boundary. The field watched helplessly as the ball cascaded over and past them.

The first over produced a single. 30 came up in the sixth over. The seventh was a maiden bowled by Aamer Hameed to Alan Lilley. 50 came in the twelfth over; the next 50 took only eight more overs. Nor did the massacre stop after lunch as Lilley now moved into top gear to complete a splendid century. McEwan, Fletcher and Hardie all made contributions and at the end of 55 overs Essex were 350 for 3, the highest score ever hit in the Benson and Hedges competition. The opening stand of 223 was also a record as was the margin of the Essex victory, 214 runs. The only Universities batsman to cause a ripple of excitement was Derek Pringle who reached a creditable 50 though the greatest disturbance he caused to the fielding side was when one of his contact lenses dropped on the wicket and the Essex players engaged in the search on hands and knees.

Trevor Bailey was to cause a stir in the cricket press, particularly up North, a few days later when he gave Essex the Team of the Week award for their three records in this match, but three competition records in one match is a considerable achievement and Trevor did not lose any friends in his home county.

Particularly pleasing for Essex had been the innings of Alan Lilley. He had received encouragement, help and coaching from older members of the side who recognised his innings as his way of repaying them. Alan had not won a place in the championship side and his innings against the Combined Universities was proof of John Lever's statement that there was now complete confidence in the reserve strength.

For the Universities the troubles did not end when David Acfield took the last two wickets. A sociable drink after Graham Gooch had received the gold award with the Commonwealth contingent led by John Ross and 'Skip' Skala in good form eased some of the pain, but when they got to the car park they discovered that Greig's car which was taking the Cambridge party back would not start.

Ray East, still troubled by injury, was not in the side for the game at Chelmsford and Reuben Herbert had been named as twelfth man for the week-end. In fact Ray came on as substitute and held a catch and travelled to Nottingham for the Sunday League game with the intention of playing, but the game was rained off.

Essex now had time to contemplate their important game with Sussex at Chelmsford on the following Wednesday. Sussex had beaten Surrey on the Saturday so that four counties, Essex, Sussex, Surrey and Northamptonshire, found themselves level on points at the top of Group C. The final round of zonal matches would decide which two counties would enter the quarter finals.

The unrelenting rain of May delayed the start at Chelmsford for an hour and a quarter, but the pitch did not appear to have suffered any ill effects. The Sussex batting, however, was totally uninspired against the unerring accuracy of the Essex bowling. Javid Miandad alone showed a willingness to play shots, but when he was three short of his fifty he drove Turner to long off where Acfield held a comfortable catch. Turner bowled his eleven overs for 16 runs and the wickets of Mendis and Miandad. When one criticises the Sussex batting for lack of aggression one must also ask what more they could have done against bowling of this calibre. With East still not fully fit, David Acfield was in the side and, bowling at a time when Sussex were desperate to increase their run rate, he again demonstrated admirable control. Sussex finished at 188 for 8.

Gooch and Lilley began as if this match were simply a continuation of the game against Combined Universities. Arnold and Imran bowled well at the outset and the ball moved about appreciably. Gooch, however, was quickly into his stride. When Phillipson came on Gooch hit him for three fours in succession. He reached 66 in 25 overs, hitting eleven fours in all, and the opening stand was worth 108 before he was caught at midwicket when he mis-hit a short ball from Spencer.

Alan Lilley batted even better than he had done on the Saturday. Using his feet to spin and seam alike, he drove sixes off Spencer, Cheatle and Barclay (twice). One of his straight sixes scattered the spectators sitting on the roof of the new buffet stand at the river end. Colin Milburn rightly gave him his first ever gold award and with Ken McEwan in fluent form victory for Essex was achieved with remarkable ease. The only person to be discomfited was Ken McEwan. He was out with only two needed to win and though he smiled apologetically at the incoming Brian Hardie, it still cost him a pint.

Essex were not concerned with the bizarre events at Worcester, but the rain in other parts of the country meant that they must wait until the Friday to know who they were to play in the quarter final. At Lord's on the Friday morning the draw was made which gave Essex the advantage of a home tie with Warwickshire, opponents whom they had no cause to fear. The game was scheduled for Ilford.

CHAPTER 6

Fireworks that would
not be Dampened

The traditional Bank Holiday matches provide one of the great attractions of the English season — the Roses Match: Middlesex and Sussex at Lord's. The first two days, at least, invariably attract large crowds and consequently bring in much needed money to county funds. The Spring Holiday of 1979 was a financial and a playing disaster.

In three days not a ball was bowled at Bristol, Derby, Lord's, Northampton, Edgbaston and The Oval, where Essex should have played Surrey. Seventeen overs were bowled at Old Trafford and the day and a half's play at Canterbury saw Hampshire have much the better of Kent and take eight points which put them on top of the championship table.

On the Sunday Essex managed to start their John Player League game at The Oval. Norbert Phillip was in fine form and Surrey were bowled out for 88 in just over 38 overs. If rain were to interrupt proceedings, Essex needed 23 in 10 overs to win. They were 25 for 1 in 9.4 overs when the players left the field because of persistent rain. As Keith Fletcher commented, Sylvester Clarke had bowled two wides so that Essex had, in fact, faced the equivalent of ten overs, but Surrey took two points in a very lucky draw.

And still it rained. In the Midlands the I.C.C. Trophy had the wettest of beginnings and the cheerful cricketers from Papua New Guinea, Bermuda, Sri Lanka, Argentina and elsewhere sat and shivered in club pavilions. It was interesting for Essex followers to note that the former Essex batsman Brian Ward was a member of the Argentinian side. Having married an Argentinian girl, Brian settled in his wife's country after he was released by Essex. Brian still coached and played and in the I.C.C. Trophy still displayed his capacity for batting rather a long time for not very many runs. He, at least, must have been used to the weather.

The bad weather was not restricted to the Midlands and none of the matches scheduled to begin on the penultimate day of May was played without interruption; indeed, the games at Sheffield and Leicester were not played at all. Though the rain stopped, there was no possibility of play on the Wednesday or Thursday at Ilford, a great disappointment to an area celebrating its centenary and one which had produced so many fine Essex players, past and present.

As no play had been possible until the last day, the game between Essex and Glamorgan was played under the rules for a one day match whereby there are only the twelve points at stake for an outright win. The batting in the session before lunch led one to believe that Glamorgan had not heard of this rule. The batsmen were completely becalmed. When Hopkins tried to cut Lever, a rare offering of a shot, he was brilliantly caught in the gully by Turner. The catch had the effect of curtailing stroke offerings even more and when lunch was taken the score was 58 for 1. 43 overs had been bowled. And we had waited two days for this.

The hundred went up in the sixty-second over with only two wickets down. The most disheartening thing about the Glamorgan batting performance was that, as they were captained by ex-Essex vice-captain Robin Hobbs, an attacking and enterprising cricketer, one had expected something better. Fletcher obviously had for he withdrew his front line bowlers from the attack and put himself on at one end and Brian Hardie at the other.

Rodney Ontong, the one Glamorgan player to remember 1979 with any joy, showed what could be done with some fine attacking shots. He made 86 before he gave a return catch to

Brian Hardie. Hardie also dismissed Llewellyn so capturing his first-ever wickets in first-class cricket. Fletcher, 'not the worst leg-break bowler in the world' as Mike Denness described him, took 3 for 44 and Glamorgan declared at 184 for 7 which had taken them 75 overs. They left Essex less than half that time, 105 minutes, in which to get the runs.

If a county side is to win any competition, positive thinking is essential. Stung by the miserable Glamorgan performance, Essex did not need any orders from their captain to tell them to go for victory. There was all to gain, nothing to lose and a few spectators who deserved some entertainment to help them forget politics, economics and the weather.

Mike Denness was caught by Ontong off Cordle with the score at 44. Gooch and McEwan then hit the remaining 141 runs that were needed in 82 minutes. The Essex innings lasted 27.3 overs. They had 5.3 overs in hand when victory came by nine wickets. Of the Glamorgan bowlers only Rodney Ontong managed to bowl a maiden. He bowled 7.3 other overs which cost 62 runs. Cordle conceded 62 in 11; Lloyd 14 in 2; Richards 36 in 6.

What picture can statistics reveal of that afternoon at Ilford? Gooch, 93 not out, two sixes, twelve fours. McEwan, 67 not out, two sixes, eight fours. But this was never a slog. Every shot was from the text book. There was never a hint of foolhardiness. Two master craftsmen were demonstrating their art in the context which was most admirably suited to their talents. Gooch, on his home ground, bludgeoned with apologetic power. McEwan drove with that lazy elegance which makes his every shot look like the offering from a god who drops some manna before his worshippers, his own cup being overfull. What few of us realised that afternoon at Ilford was that we were seeing the first performance of an act that was to be repeated at Lord's in six weeks' time. What we also did not know when we heard that evening that Essex's win had taken them to the top of the championship table with a lead of ten points was that they were to remain in that position for the rest of the season.

CHAPTER 7

John Lever and the
Month of June

June was to be dominated for most cricket followers by the Prudential World Cup, but for Essex supporters it was a month of great significance for the County.

On Sunday, 3 June, the England party for the World Cup was announced. Gooch, the most exciting batsman in the country at this time, was an automatic choice. So, too, we felt, was John Lever. When the England selectors disclosed their fourteen chosen players, twelve of the players who had toured Australia the previous winter were in the side, plus Larkins and Gatting. The name of John Lever was not among the fourteen announced. His exclusion, and the inclusion of Gatting, will remain as one of the most incomprehensible selection decisions of all time. It was a decision that was to be cursed by counties other than Essex.

The news of the team came when Essex were engaged in one of their made for television horror matches; this time the recipients of largesse were Lancashire. Bob Willis, in his book *Diary of a Cricket Season*, forwards the opinion that the England side is better for having John Lever in the squad because he is such an eminently fine person and good for morale. There are few who would disagree with this opinion. To have the reputation of being one of the most amiable of men has its drawbacks, however. People begin to believe that you accept any hurt or rebuttal that life gives you with a smile and a shrug of the shoulders, that you are 'as one in suff'ring all that suffers nothing.' John Lever had taken 'Fortune's buffets and rewards' with equal thanks, but he was deeply hurt by his omission from the World Cup squad. It took him twenty-four hours to frame his reply.

The Saturday had again seen Ken McEwan in scintillating form. He followed his innings against Glamorgan of the previous day with 88 in just under two hours. Once more it was that indolent swing of the bat that sent the ball straight back over the bowler's head. Twice he lifted Arrowsmith into the crowd, eleven times he pierced the field to reach the boundary. After Gooch and Denness had gone for 65, McEwan and Fletcher added 50, the skipper scored 8. Then Brian Hardie joined the South African in a stand of 76 before McEwan provided Reidy with one of his rare wickets in first-class cricket. McEwan played no stroke at a straight ball and was bowled, a bewildering anti-climax to two hours of batting magic.

The sun was shining and Brian Hardie found immediate touch. His powerful forearms and his eagerness to move onto the front foot soon had him scoring freely off the Lancashire attack. Turner and Smith joined him in useful stands and the four bonus points came with ease. As soon as Hardie reached his hundred which he did by turning Lee to fine leg, Fletcher declared. Neil Smith was 30 not out, showing once more what a valuable hitter he is. After three quick overs in the gloom the umpires decided play should end for the day and Lancashire were 9 for 0 facing the Essex score of 339 for 6.

There was general sympathy for John Lever as Essex took the field on Monday morning. Even the sultry atmosphere and the greenness of the wicket were on his side. In his second over of the day he bowled Wood when the Lancashire opener played forward half heartedly. The ball now began to swing menacingly. By the end of his sixth over of the morning Lever had taken five wickets while conceding eleven runs. Behind the wicket was a ring of fielders in vulture-like poses and the Lancashire batsmen, mesmerised, edged the ball to them almost wilfully. Lancashire out for 84, Lever 7 for 27.

They fared little better when they followed on, moving from

120 for 5 to 123 all out. David Acfield took the last four wickets in eleven balls without conceding a run. Essex had won by an innings and 132 runs inside two days, John Lever had made his point and their lead at the top of the championship table over Hampshire had been stretched to 26 points. Their next concern was the Benson and Hedges quarter final.

The match against Warwickshire was switched to Chelmsford. There were several rumours circulating as to the reason for this change; one was that vandals had driven across the strip on motor bikes, another that Ilford third eleven had played on the wicket when it was wet. Whatever the reason, Warwickshire came to Chelmsford on a fine day and play started on time.

There was an air of confidence as Gooch and Lilley strode out to open the Essex innings. The crowded Chelmsford ground bubbled excitedly. The form of Gooch, Lilley and McEwan, the two fine victories at Ilford, the bowling of Lever, Turner and Phillip, the fielding and catching, the pleasure at being at the top of the county championship, all these things gave the Essex supporters a buoyancy and the team a sense of purposeful energy.

The start shattered the mood of optimism. All at sea, Lilley fenced nervously two or three times before touching Ferreira to Amiss. 2 for 1, last man 0. Willis bowled his first six overs for 1 run. He did not bowl as well in any other game that summer. Of the first 12 overs, seven were maidens. Only nineteen runs came in the first ten overs. McEwan and Gooch batted determinedly, but never grimly.

In the summer of 1979, Graham Gooch reaped the harvest of experience. After the traumatic Test debut, the two years of uncertainty that followed, the careful re-introduction to the England side, the hard lessons of Australia, he had emerged a wiser person. The excitement of the flashing blade had always been his, now he had acquired watchful defence and the ability to accumulate runs at a steady pace. The promising youth was now a mature man.

Well as Willis bowled in that opening spell, he did not take a

wicket and Gooch and McEwan, the latter less feverish in his
start than at other times, moved into the second phase of the
game with dignity and grace.

The danger when the tension is eased is that concentration
may lapse, but Gooch and McEwan had prised the initiative
from the Warwickshire attack and now their concentration was
channelled into aggression. McEwan moved effortlessly into his
shots. Now the bats began to swing in a wider arc and the crowd
relaxed as the ball regularly hit the boundary boards. In truth,
the Warwickshire second line bowling was no match for batting
of this quality. The hundred was up in 90 minutes and just as
McEwan reached his fifty he drove a little too lazily at Oliver
who took a fine catch diving to his left. But there was to be no
respite for Warwickshire. Fletcher was immediately busy
scampering for runs. He kept pace with Gooch while 90 were
added. Brian Hardie left quickly, but the occasion was well to
the liking of Keith Pont who drove mightily, 22 in 5 overs.

Just after he had completed his hundred in the 49th over,
Gooch drove the ball back head high at Steve Perryman who
could not hold the offering. His six more overs at the wicket
were to cost Warwickshire another 37 runs from his bat. He was
lbw to Willis on the second ball of the last over. He had hit a
massive six into the car park and nineteen times he had found
the boundary. His score was 138 and as he walked from the
wicket the crowd rose in tribute. It was no perfunctory gesture
from supporters following a fashion; it was the awe and
reverence demanded by great art.

In those closing overs every Warwickshire player, bar bowler
and wicket-keeper, was round the boundary, but still the ball
reached the fence for four. 97 runs were scored in the last ten
overs. Three overs from Ferreira cost 45 runs; five overs from
Willis cost 31.

To win Warwickshire needed to score 272, a total which had
only been achieved once by a side batting second in the competition.

Amiss and Smith began well against Phillip and Lever, both

of whom were slow to settle. Turner came into the attack, bowling from the river end. Amiss tried to turn a ball to leg that lifted just a little and Smith took a beautifully judged, unacrobatic catch as the ball moved away down the leg-side. Two runs later Whitehouse, in a fever of indecision, was run out at the bowler's end. Kallicharran was off the mark quickly, but flashed at Turner outside the off stump and Smith was gleefully throwing the ball in the air: 36 for 3. At tea the contest was already settled.

Some brave batting from Smith, Oliver and Humpage brought Warwickshire to within 44 of the Essex total, but there was no disputing that Essex were in the Benson and Hedges semi-finals for the second time in the competition's history. They were to meet Yorkshire at Chelmsford in an all-ticket match.

The problem that now confronted Fletcher was to maintain the state of confident exuberance in his side without allowing it to develop into over-excitement. Gooch went off to join the England side and was to be one of the three outstanding batsmen in the Prudential World Cup tournament. Essex wished him well, but attention was focussed on the Schweppes County Championship. Gooch would not be available again for Essex until the Gillette Cup game at Old Trafford on 27 June. Before that date Essex would meet Leicestershire, Warwickshire, Somerset, Derbyshire and Kent in the Schweppes County Championship. Soberly, amid the euphoria at leading the championship table and being in the Benson and Hedges semi-final, came the realisation that success would depend on how well the side did without the batsman who, in the first six weeks of the season, had been the most prominent in the country.

It was a surprise to most that McEvoy, and not Lilley, was chosen to replace Gooch in the team to meet Leicestershire at Chelmsford. McEvoy had made his debut in 1976 at the age of 20. He had played nine first-class games in three years, had hit two fifties and had always looked a very good player. Since his debut he had been a student at Borough Road College, but his love was cricket and his second eleven record was magnificent. In selecting McEvoy, Fletcher and his advisers were stating that the team choices were thoughtful and guided by the desire to win, and not by sentiment.

McEvoy did a splendid job and helped Denness in an opening stand of 63, but the middle order crumpled badly; McEwan, Fletcher, Turner and Phillip scored only five altogether and Essex were 157 for 6.

In the final analysis of a successful season, all innings, all games, are seen as important, yet perhaps there is one moment when the destiny of a side hangs in the balance. Had Essex faltered against Leicestershire that afternoon when for the first time they were without Graham Gooch, it is possible that the optimism, the belief that winning the title could be achieved, would have given way to the former sense of resignation to finishing second. Happily, in Mike Denness, Essex had a man who was both used to winning and believed in winning. He knew the responsibility that now rested with him and he responded with his first hundred of the season.

He and Hardie had doubled the score, but when the sixth wicket fell, two batting bonus points looked the most that Essex could hope for. Neil Smith had other ideas and when Denness finally fell to Shuttleworth for 122, Essex were only one short of their third batting point. It would appear to be considered if not slang, at least a cliché, to say a batsman 'carved up an attack', but that is exactly how Neil Smith bats. He carves the ball with a short, vigorous, immensely powerful thrust that sends fieldsmen scurrying helplessly in all directions. If you do not dismiss the man, you suffer two hours of torture and become the objects of the audience's hilarity. Leicestershire did not dismiss him. Essex 303 for 9, Neil Smith 90 not out. He hit his highest score of the season at the time when it was needed most.

Play had ended early on the Saturday. Leicestershire passed 150 with only three wickets down, but they were checked by John Lever who took the wickets of Davison, Tolchard, Balderstone and Cook in four overs. Essex grabbed a lead of 71, Lever had 6 for 76 and Turner four catches.

The second innings started badly for Essex. They were 10 for 3, finished the day at 48 for 3 with McEwan in control, but the prospects for the last day were not bright.

Fletcher's thinking at this stage was entirely positive. For Essex a draw had as little merit as defeat. They would attack the bowling and press for victory. This they did. Hardie acted as the foundation of the innings while everyone else was ordered to go for his shots. They scored at the rate of a run a minute. Turner hit two sixes in a thrilling 48 and they were all out at lunch for 181 so that Leicestershire needed 253 to win.

Turner and Lever, asked during the interval what they felt about their chances of forcing victory, responded with the conviction that Essex needed some sun to help dry the wicket and give the bowlers a chance. The sun did not come, but the wickets did.

Phillip achieved the initial breakthrough and Lever then swung the ball and moved it off the seam to the complete discomfort of the Leicestershire batsmen. By mid-afternoon they were 66 for 7 and had not Turner been no-balled as he bowled Davison, their position would have been even worse, for Davison it was who gave the Leicestershire innings some respectability in an aggressive stand with Shuttleworth. Davison swung once too often at Phillip and was bowled, and Shuttleworth went the same way. Inevitably, it was Lever who finished the innings with sixteen of the last twenty overs still remaining. He had taken 7 for 41, 13 for 117 in the match, a career best. Hampshire and Northants had drawn. Essex went to Birmingham with a lead of 40 points in the Schweppes County Championship.

Though they had reached the quarter-finals of the Benson and Hedges by winning all four of their zonal matches, the only team to do this, Warwickshire had done nothing to suggest that they would be anything other than one of the weaker county sides of 1979. A side weakened by the calls of England and

West Indies for the Prudential World Cup was further depleted by injuries, but it is doubtful if Warwickshire at full strength and in top form would have been a match for Essex in mid-June.

The atmosphere at Edgbaston was humid and there was John Lever in golden vein, the artist at the peak of performance with all the subtleties and virtuosities accumulated over the years striving towards a perfection which by the law of nature must ultimately be denied him. In his third over he straightened a delivery to trap Smith lbw. Whitehouse was faced by the same ball — or was it? No, the angle of delivery, the flight were adjusted slightly as the Warwickshire captain realised too late, his off stump knocked back.

Lloyd should have gone twice, both times dropped by Turner off the luckless Phillip. Four catches in the first innings against Leicestershire had been snapped up by Turner; the gods of cricket distribute gifts and punishments in equal measure. Turner sought his own revenge and the left-handed Lloyd edged his outswinger to McEvoy at slip.

In the afternoon John Lever destroyed the Warwickshire innings. Amiss had batted with caution and passed an excellent fifty as he struggled to hold the side together, but Lever slanted the ball across him, took the edge of the bat and McEvoy held the catch in the gully. A few balls earlier Oliver was brilliantly caught by Hardie at short leg, diving to his left and taking the ball inches from the ground. Hardie took 30 catches in 1979 and his contribution to the side as specialist fielder at 'Boot Hill' is immeasurable, for even when he was not taking catches, his very presence inhibited opponents and brought about their downfall in other areas.

In a spell of fifteen overs in the afternoon John Lever took five wickets for 16 runs. After tea he dismissed Steve Perryman, Turner bowled Savage and the Warwickshire innings was at an end. Lever had taken 8 for 49, so bettering his previous 8 for 127 against Gloucestershire in 1976.

McEvoy fell in Perryman's first over and Ray East came in as night watchman. 11 for 1 off five overs.

Any hopes Warwickshire may have had of gaining quick advantage on the Thursday morning evaporated in a spate of boundaries. Ray East hit 7 fours in his 49, Mike Denness 6 in his 34. Then came Ken McEwan.

Warwickshire's troubles with injuries were worsened when Steve Perryman, their most experienced bowler, was taken to hospital for an X-ray on a badly bruised ankle. Cynically, one might suggest he was better in hospital than he would have been at Edgbaston that day.

It is one of the sadnesses of cricket that some of the greatest and most memorable moments of the noblest of games take place when few eyes are watching and when television cameras are not there to record them for posterity. In 54 overs McEwan and Fletcher added 219 for the fourth wicket. In an aggressive mood, with his shots in full flight, Keith Fletcher is both a batsman of beauty and a rapid scorer, but Ken McEwan out-scored him two to one. McEwan's hundred came in two and a quarter hours. His second hundred came in an hour and forty minutes. He was 208 not out when rain stopped play and he had hit 5 sixes and 22 fours. He gave one chance, to Amiss at slip, when he had scored 22.

There are some batsmen who breathe power as they walk to the wicket. Their muscles ripple. Their shirt buttons strain as if keeping in check some energy which is eager for release. Procter and Greenidge are of this school as was Keith Boyce. They hit a ball viciously. Ken McEwan is not of this type. He walks to the wicket lazily, amost unwillingly. When he drives the emphasis is on beauty, rather than power. The arrogance in his batting is an arrogance born of elegance and aristocracy. A display of strength for its own sake from him would be a breach of manners. Two successive deliveries from Clifford were lifted nonchalantly over long-off for six. There was no venom in the shots, yet they were struck with a force that was sufficient to worry the scorers close to whom the ball landed each time. Perhaps rain was the only thing that could have brought an end to his innings.

Fletcher declared at the overnight score and what followed had about it an air of inevitability. Lever bowled Amiss at 10, but Warwickshire went in to lunch at 97 for 2. An hour and forty minutes after lunch they were all out for 134. Ray East had had his best spell of the season and John Lever had taken 5 for 38 which gave him 13 for 87 in the match, so beating his career-best figures of the previous match. In five days he had taken 26 wickets for 204 runs. Kent and Somerset had suffered from rain at Dartford, and one point was all that came from the match. Essex now led the Schweppes County Championship by 60 points; they had passed the hundred mark.

Not surprisingly Lever was named as the *Sunday Telegraph*—Victoria Wine Cricketer of the Week, the fourth Essex player to collect a crate of Moët and Chandon since the season began. For Essex it was a champagne year in every sense.

The game at Bath brought together the two sides considered by many people to be the best in England. Somerset batted dourly, but Essex still took their four bowling points. Acfield and Turner bore the brunt of the bowling. McEvoy again left early, stumped — the impetuosity of youth. East was once more at number three, night watchman.

The Sunday interlude was once more like something out of a Mervyn Peake novel, but sanity had returned by Monday and Ray East consolidated his claim to be the best night watchman in the business. With Denness he added 82, with McEwan 63. He was out shortly after lunch caught at square leg off Moseley.

McEwan's form was just what it had been at Edgbaston. His off-side shots were a joy and another century seemed to be on the way. In one over from Breakwell he straight drove a glorious six and then pulled him next ball for another six, then concentration faltered and he swept lazily to be bowled. It was Brian Hardie who saw Essex to the fourth batting point though it was Norbert Phillip who reached the three hundred mark in the final over of the innings.

Phillip it was who put Essex on the way to success in the second innings when he had Rose caught at slip by Fletcher.

Slocombe, Denning and Roebuck had joined their skipper in the pavilion before the close, and once more Essex were in sight of victory and another twenty points.

Kitchen was caught behind off Lever early on the Tuesday morning, 63 for 5, and victory for Essex now seemed a formality. Somerset are a team of quality, however, and Marks, Dredge and Breakwell effected a fine recovery.

Essex needed 260 to win in 142 minutes, but any thought of victory was quickly dispersed when Denness and McEvoy were out with only 11 scored. Worse was to come and in the end Phillip and East were thankful to hold out against Hallam Moseley, only in the side because Garner was with the West Indies team. Moseley took 5 for 18 and Essex had been taught the dangers of over-confidence.

Kent had beaten Gloucestershire by an innings and ominously moved into second place though the Essex lead was still a substantial one, 56 points.

McEvoy had failed twice at Bath while Alan Lilley was hitting a century for the second eleven, and it was not surprising to find that Lilley was preferred as Denness's opening partner. One other change was made in that Pont returned to the exclusion of Acfield, presumably because it was felt that seam rather than spin would be needed to dispose of Derbyshire at Chelmsford.

This judgement seemed correct when Lever, Phillip and Turner had Derbyshire staggering at 53 for 6, but three Derbyshire players hit fifties and their innings lasted until the 98th over and reached 258. Alan Lilley was caught without scoring and Essex went home at 8 for 1 with Ray East yet again batting at number three.

John Lever had taken another five wickets, but following the second innings debacle at Bath this first day's play against Derbyshire had raised feelings of uncertainty. There was the suspicion that we were seeing the beginning of the Essex crack, that collapse which had attended all their previous attempts to win a trophy. There was no question of Fletcher calling a team

meeting and asking everyone to try harder. It was not possible
for a team to give more than Essex had been giving. It was more
a question of belief, of shrugging aside yesterday and concen-
trating on to-day. This was exactly what Essex did on Thursday,
21 June.

Ray East batted sensibly until caught behind with the score
at 39. In the next 25 overs Denness and McEwan added 131
runs, and Ken McEwan scored 109 of them. His hundred was
reached in 85 minutes, the fastest of the season to date. As well
as the eloquent drives, he played some pulls of uncharacteris-
tic viciousness. In all he was at the wicket for 47 overs while
239 runs were scored; he scored 185 of them. This was an
innings to challenge Jessopian legend for he scored 134 runs in
boundaries: 29 fours and 3 sixes, the two off Steele of massive
proportions. He was finally caught at mid-wicket when he mis-
hit Kirsten and skied the ball to Steele.

Technically his innings against Derbyshire was the equal of
his innings against Warwickshire the previous week; psychologi-
cally it was of even greater value to his side. It was a decisive
and exhilarating statement that Essex believed in winning. Pont
(77) and Turner (43) batted splendidly in the closing overs as
Essex declared when Pont was out on the second ball of the
100th over. The score was 435 for 9. Lever then dismissed
Anderson before bad light brought an early close, but the
memory of Ken McEwan was what Essex supporters took home
with them that night; that was an innings to remember.

The game was over by mid-afternoon on Friday. The ball
seamed appreciably and the Essex bowlers and fielders were in
voracious mood. Lever and Phillip each had four wickets, and
Turner was particularly unlucky to be rewarded with only one
wicket as he beat the bat consistently.

Middlesex had held out against Kent — match drawn. The
Essex lead was 69 points from Nottinghamshire who had played
two games fewer. All seemed right in the world again.

Not surprisingly, Ken McEwan was the fifth Essex recipient
of the weekly champagne. In the first eight weeks of the

Sunday Telegraph—Victoria Wine award Essex had claimed the prize on all but three occasions. All this, of course, was dwarfed by the Prudential World Cup Final between England and West Indies at Lord's. The injury to Willis and the use of Boycott—Gooch—Larkins as the fifth bowler in the England side reopened the wound over selection. It is as difficult in hindsight as it was at the time to comprehend the choice of Gatting, who did not play a game, instead of Lever. At the end of the season there was more than one member of the England side who remained as perplexed as the present writer.

The World Cup Final dominated all events and it was a pity that the Essex game on the beautiful Tunbridge Wells ground should clash with it. It was a greater shame that rain should decree that there should be no more play in the game after the first day when Chris Tavare hit a splendid hundred and made Kent, and Essex, supporters wonder why he was not at Lord's. Luck was with Essex, however, in that Leicestershire pulled off a surprising win over Nottinghamshire who were lying second in the table.

With interest now moving to the Gillette Cup, Essex had a rest period from the Schweppes County Championship, a period when they would have to sit back and watch their rivals struggle to close the gap which they had opened up at the top of the table. The lead was 67 points at the end of June, a month in which John Lever had taken 53 wickets. Alan Ealham still expressed the view that Kent would retain the championship, but there were many who believed that the title already belonged to Essex. Essex supporters knew from past experience that there was still a long way to go.

CHAPTER 8

An Ambition Realised

For a team with such a good reputation in limited over cricket, Essex have a poor record in the Gillette Cup. The match at Old Trafford did nothing to improve that record. The wicket was taking a considerable amount of spin by mid-afternoon and, justifiably, Essex lodged a complaint after the game, but, in truth, their efforts at containment during the Lancashire innings had not been very successful.

Though undoubtedly there was disappointment at going out of the Gillette Cup in the first round, Essex players were not too unhappy at the fixture list which allowed them calm preparation for the Benson and Hedges semi-final. Even though they were not engaged in a three-day game, they could not be overtaken in the Schweppes County Championship and a home game in the John Player League against Kent was the perfect sharpener for the encounter with Yorkshire.

John Lever and Graham Gooch were in the M.C.C. side to meet India at Lord's. Neither distinguished himself though, when Brearley was injured, Lever did find himself captaining the side. Much to everybody's surprise Essex annihilated Kent on the Sunday and the semi-final was faced with just the right amount of confidence.

The day of the semi-final at Chelmsford was beautiful. The sun shone. There was a suggestion of cloud, but blue dominated the sky, and the ground was packed to capacity with good-humoured people.

Knowing their side's inhibitions about chasing a target, Essex supporters were apprehensive when Fletcher won the toss and asked Yorkshire to bat. The fact that Yorkshire were without Boycott and that Old, too, had been a doubtful starter because of injury may have influenced his decision, but the real reasoning was Lever's form and the belief that the ball would move about in the pre-lunch session. Neither reason was justified by subsequent events.

Whatever problems Yorkshire had had with injuries seemed as nothing when Lumb and Hampshire got into their stride. The ball did not appear to deviate in the slightest and runs came freely. The first ten overs produced 41 runs. There was one close call for lbw, one quick follow-through by John Lever at an attempted run out, but the early session belonged entirely to the visitors.

Stuart Turner and Keith Pont replaced Lever and Phillip and the brake was applied, but Pont erred in direction and conceded 22 in two overs. Hampshire hit Pont massively into the crowd at long off. Runs were beginning to come at six an over. Hampshire reached his 50. The hundred partnership was acclaimed vociferously by the Yorkshire contingent. East threatened to curb the scoring so Hampshire stepped out to drive. He hit high for the long-on boundary, the longest boundary on the ground, and Turner took a splendid running catch. Yorkshire had scored 107 in the first 29 overs before losing a wicket. In the 26 remaining overs they were to score only 66 runs and lose 9 wickets.

The original ball had certainly not swung at all. It had gone out of shape and the replacement had swung a little, but this did not excuse the Yorkshire collapse. Sharp and Athey were completely ill at ease. Sharp twice aimed and missed and then went lbw to Phillip. Athey was grotesque, chopped at East and was bowled: 114 for 3 and most of the eight thousand people lunched far better than they had expected at 12.30.

Bewilderingly the Yorkshire youngsters had thrown away the advantage a splendid start had given them. Soon after lunch Love swung impetuously at Pont and was caught by McEwan, comfortably, at square leg.

Whilst Lumb was at the wicket Yorkshire still breathed with hope, but in the 46th over his splendid innings came to an end when he was yorked by Phillip who had now discovered length, direction and fire.

Bairstow, surely too high at number six, fretted painfully for quick runs. Impatient with Sidebottom, he charged up the wicket when his partner drove to mid-on and Pont's underarm throw knocked off a bail before he could regain his ground. He left muttering over his shoulder, but at least he had made 10 and only he and Stevenson reached double figures after the two openers. Sidebottom went to Turner, Lever dismissed both Stevenson and Carrick. Old managed only one run in the last over and, with unbelievable joy, Essex needed only 174 to win.

It is with amazement and disgust that economists count the number of people who attend mid-week sporting events and suggest that they should be at work, stabilising the country's financial affairs. Essex supporter Geoff Freeman might have agreed with them when, after listening to comments around him, he commented in the period between innings, 'There are eight thousand people here to-day and I am the only one who seems to have taken an official day's holiday.' One poster emphasised Geoff's observation. On a white sheet black letters announced 'Tom Brown is not at the dentist's — he's here' — an arrow marked the spot.

The collapse of their batting had not dampened the spirits of the Yorkshire supporters though they were in less buoyant mood than they had been earlier in the day. Nevertheless, as they sipped their ale at least one nodded knowingly 'We've got 'em on the board. You've still got to get there.'

Gooch took two through the off-side in Old's opening over. Lilley faced Stevenson's first delivery. He hung out his bat and Bairstow and the slips erupted gleefully.

McEwan was in a state of feverish nervousness. He flashed wildly at Stevenson, but Bairstow dropped a hard catch down the leg side. McEwan pulled a frenetic four, off drove another. Just as he seemed to be settling and Essex pulling away to victory, McEwan waved his bat at Sidebottom and Bairstow claimed his second catch: 42 for 2.

Fletcher played with assurance and then suddenly cut wildly at Stevenson, now operating from the Writtle End, and Sidebottom held a stinging catch in the gully and left the field for repairs.

Hardie applied the common sense of the Scot and with Gooch batting with confidence and control, if a little luck, Essex began to move into a position of ascendancy.

With Gooch on 49 and the score at 99, that one run short of the sense of ultimate security, Sidebottom dropped one short. Gooch hooked and Bairstow, leaping high to his left, took a catch of spectacular quality.

Still Hardie batted well; positive in defence, but ever looking for the run. In 24 overs at the crease he gave the innings a look of permanence, then he drove at Sidebottom and Bairstow took his fourth catch of the innings; 112 for 5 and the game now tilted slightly in Yorkshire's favour.

Pont and Phillip, to their everlasting credit, curbed their natural tendencies to swing the bat. Again Essex edged closer. Momentarily Phillip forgot himself, hit out at Carrick and was caught at mid-off: 139 for 6.

Turner joined Pont. Turner had taken a fine running catch to alter the course of the match; he had been the first Essex bowler to curb the Yorkshire scoring; now he was asked to show the complete all-rounder's skill with a batting display that could put Essex on the brink of victory. He played determined defence, but looked always for the single, never giving advantage to the fielding side. He cajoled his younger partner, but Pont needed no telling, engaged as he was upon what was probably his finest, certainly his most important, innings for Essex. Hampshire took the calculated gamble and threw Old into the attack, allowing him to finish his quota of overs. Pont and Turner stood firm.

Cooper bowled from the river end so leaving the riddle as to who would bowl the last over from the Writtle end. The field was moved in. Pont tried to drive over the top and Love took the catch at mid-on. He had scored 36, but, amid their disappointment, the crowd rose to him as if it were a double century.

Smith came out to face the county of his birth with five runs needed to win and nine balls to go. Turner hit a single. Smith took guard determinedly and did not take a long glance around the field. He knew his opponents. Cooper bowled just outside the off stump and Smith hit a hard, sweet shot which skimmed the turf all the way to the off-side boundary square with the wicket, and Essex had won. The tension which had gripped the crowd since early morning dissolved into cheers, laughter, back-slapping and handshakes.

Turner hugged Neil Smith and ran from the field waving his bat. Words he spoke at a quiet dinner party after a disappointing defeat a few years previously were recalled. 'If we could only get to Lord's once and just play in a final in front of all those people. I wouldn't mind if we won or not, but just to get there.' His dream had been realised, but one felt that neither he, nor the others, would be content now with being runners-up.

The bars were crowded with good-humoured celebrators. Yorkshire supporters, lovers and knowers of the game, said with truth, 'We gave you a run for it — and a fright.'

For Essex followers it seemed an occasion for more than handshakes, an un-English embrace.

Players joined their families and friends. We congratulated Graham Gooch though suggested that Essex had made hard work of it.

'You know what we're like chasing runs, but we got there. I've only been playing five years so I'm lucky. Eastie, Fletch and Stuart are crying in the dressing-room upstairs. They've waited all their cricket lives for this.'

There may be protests that we all take this lovely game too seriously, that we give to it more emotion and commitment than it warrants, but such protesters have never probed beneath the surface. We never forget that cricket is a game, that there are things more fundamental to the act of living and dying, but in a world where every day someone murders or is murdered in the name of some satanic cause, there is a refreshing breath of sanity in intellect and emotion spent in the honesty of physical endeavour.

All of us bring an agony of concern to the job we do; few of us derive from it such an emotional and aesthetic sense of fulfilment as the professional cricketer. The secret of the success of Essex is that the players have never forgotten that they are both privileged and lucky to be earning their living in the way that they do, and they continue to enjoy it while they can.

CHAPTER 9

Southend Week—The Form of Champions

The victory over Yorkshire in the semi-final of the Benson and Hedges Cup was the most important in the history of Essex in that it had put them in the final of a competition for the first time.

There is always the danger of a decline after the scaling of a height, emotional or otherwise. Two days' rest, which meant joining in activities for Stuart Turner's benefit, was followed by Southend week and a return to seeking the most coveted prize in English cricket, the Schweppes County Championship.

Southchurch Park is the least attractive ground on which Essex play, but it has a sense of space and that is very necessary for a side with people clamouring to see them.

The first opponents in Southend week were Sussex, a side rich in potential, a little disappointing in performance. Imran and Arnold can pose threats, but Gooch and Denness were in regal mood and Sussex were put to the sword; 170 came for the first wicket. Denness hit a chanceless hundred, taking over the leading role from Gooch, and Fletcher, who himself hit an unbeaten fifty, declared in the hundredth over at 338 for 5.

Outside the team which had beaten Yorkshire there were two contenders for places in the final — Mike Denness and David Acfield. Denness had been omitted from John Player League and Benson and Hedges games at the outset as a policy decision, in order to blood Alan Lilley. Alan, a modest and dedicated young man, had taken his chance with splendid innings in the Benson and Hedges zonal matches against Combined Universities and Sussex, since when his form had faltered.

First-class cricket is an exacting business. A player can make an instant impression as Brian Hardie had done in 1974 and 1975, but then the bush telegraph spreads the news of the discovery of an Achilles heel, and the young professional must start again, working on the eradication of the vulnerability. Lilley had reached this point in his career, the point of rehabilitation.

Denness's value to Essex was that after years at the very highest peak of his profession his appetite for the game was as big as ever. He still wanted to play. He still wanted to succeed and to be part of any success. At Southchurch Park his innings gave notice of his desire.

On the Sunday Gooch hit his highest John Player League innings of the season and Essex won by nine runs. John Lever was named in the twelve for the First Cornhill Test against India.

The following day Lever took seven wickets as Sussex went from their Saturday overnight total of 28 for 0 to 143 all out, and, following on, 146 for 6. Phillipson and Imran delayed matters a little on the last day and Essex had to bat again to score 12 runs which they did in two overs. The pace attack had again spurred Essex to victory; Phillip had match figures of 8 for 97; Lever 7 for 113; and Turner 4 for 46.

Whilst Essex were achieving this win, a few miles along the A. 13, at the Thames Board Mills Ground at Purfleet, Essex Schools' under-15 side were entertaining Welsh Schools, nine of whom were later to play against England. Essex were 36 for 3 when Barry Lemmon joined Paul Prichard. Both boys were playing in a year group one year older than themselves, both had already won their county badges. Two and a half hours later Essex declared at 263 for 3. Paul Prichard was 187 not out. It was the highest team score ever hit at this level and the highest individual score. Essex cricket was in good hands.

It is essential to the health of a county side that youngsters at school aspire to playing for their county. Gooch, Lever, Lilley and Pont were all products of Essex Schools' cricket and of the masters and coaches who give hours of their time. Haydn Davies, Peter Green, 'Sam' Coster, Jim Bowden and the rest have chosen, shaped and advised Essex sides at school level for several years, and driven them, at their own expense, to all parts of the country. Few people, even at county administration level, realise how much of the success of Essex is owed to them and to coaches like Bill Morris and Doug Pont. Essex desperately needs to follow the lead of that other thriving county, Somerset, and have an automatic committee place for a schools' representative.

The second match in the Southend week saw Nottinghamshire as visitors. Lever had been called to Edgbaston as replacement for the injured Old, so Essex lost his services while he carried the drinks tray.

Nottinghamshire had been challenging Essex as strongly as anyone for the championship lead so that the meeting was seen as a vital one. The wicket had been shaved and was expected to take spin. Acfield came into the side for Lever though the name of Gary Sainsbury had been mentioned for the first time. Sainsbury, another product of Essex Schools, had enjoyed great success for Wanstead in the Truman League and looks very much like John Lever in style. He had taken 8 for 8 in a second-team game against Middlesex and had become a serious contender for a first-team place.

Denness played another handsome innings as he and Lilley gave Essex a good start, but after that everybody got a few and nobody got enough. By tea Essex were out for 240. Bore and Hemmings, the two spinners, had done most of the bowling for Notts.

The evening session was bad for Essex. Fletcher put down a straightforward slip catch off Turner's bowling. Smith should have stumped Smedley off East who did not bowl well. Rice hit East into the Access tent and though Phillip had yorked Harris for 9, Notts finished the day at 100 for 2.

The second day continued the tale of Essex woe. Rice took his score to 86 before becoming one of East's four victims, and

Norbert Phillip. It was his arrival that helped to turn Essex into a championship-winning side *(Sporting Pictures (UK) Ltd)*

Alan Lilley *(right)* and Mike McEvoy *(below)*: young men with a future of success *(Sporting Pictures (UK) Ltd)*

Right Neil Smith. In the daily grind of first-class cricket few wicket-keepers can equal him in consistent application *(Sporting Pictures (UK) Ltd)*

Below Senior members of the cast relax in training: Keith Fletcher, Ray East, John Lever, Mike Denness *(Sporting Pictures (UK) Ltd)*

Above Keith Pont: a maturing cricketer of great power and potential
(Patrick Eagar)
Opposite Stuart Turner — benefit year and bristling with endeavour
(Sporting Pictures (UK) Ltd)

John Lever — the most successful bowler in English cricket in 1979. A
young man of fresh and honest charm, and 'an international cricketer
by any standard' *(Patrick Eagar)*

Mike Denness: *eminence grise* and youthful fire *(Patrick Eagar)*

Ken McEwan square-cuts Swarbrook for four to reach his hundred against
Derbyshire in eighty-five minutes, Chelmsford, 21 June
(Sporting Pictures (UK) Ltd)

the Notts innings ground on, using the overs which Essex had not occupied and building a lead of 60. When Essex batted again wickets fell regularly. At the close they were 111 for 5, 51 ahead. Fletcher was 41 not out and Phillip 11 not out. It seemed certain that Friday would see their first championship defeat of the season.

When Fletcher chopped a catch to Mackintosh in the gully in the third over of the morning, with only two runs added to the overnight score, it seemed that Essex would not even be able to hold out until lunch time.

Though he sometimes wastes the opportunity of improving his batting average when there are easy runs to be had, as at Edgbaston, Turner is never one to fail when his side is in need. He and Norbert Phillip decided, characteristically, that the best form of defence was attack. Pace and spin were treated with equal aggression. The threatening Bore (he took 5 for 79) was hit for 14 in one over by Turner, including a superb straight six. Phillip, too, was in belligerent mood and the pair added 66 before the West Indian fell to Bore. Smith and East went quickly, but Acfield joined Turner in a last-wicket stand of immense value.

Like most bowlers David Acfield considers himself a better batsman than either his position in the order or his average would suggest. Partnerships with Stuart Turner have a habit of bringing the best from him — he once stayed with Stuart at Swansea while the all-rounder reached his hundred — and this was no exception.

Acfield relied mainly on defence, but he struck two crashing fours, and Turner continued to attack. Turner had one 'life' on the long-on boundary, but refused to be inhibited. On the last ball before lunch, with Hadlee bowling, Acfield attempted to fend off a ball that lifted and trod on his wicket. He had scored 10. Turner was 68 not out. They had added 42 for the last wicket, a stand which, in the context of the match, was to have profound significance.

Nottinghamshire began batting after lunch needing 170 to

win. Phillip and Turner bowled only eleven overs in the innings and the spinners, East and Acfield, were soon in action. Harris and Hassan started confidently. Harris fell lbw to East at 40, but Smedley joined Hassan in easing Notts towards victory.

With the score at 87, Acfield pushed one through Smedley's uncertain stroke and bowled him. In his next over he turned one sharply enough for Brian Hardie to snap up yet another chance at 'Boot Hill'. The wickets had come shortly after the spinners had changed ends and now it was East's turn to strike as Rice played too soon, deceived by the flight, and the bowler took the return catch. 108 for 4 at tea, Notts lost four wickets on the resumption for the addition of only two runs. Curzon struck a couple of blows, but the Nottinghamshire cause was now beyond hope. Bore went lbw to Acfield and Hacker fell to the same bowler when Hardie took another brilliant catch inches from the bat; 123 all out and Essex had won by 46 runs.

After tea the last six Nottinghamshire wickets had fallen in 12 overs and 2 balls whilst only 15 runs were scored. Both spinners had returned their best figures of the season, East 5 for 56; Acfield 5 for 28. Acfield had bowled 23.2 overs, 12 of which had been maidens. One was reminded of Norman Cuff's famous after-dinner quip 'David Acfield should be spinning for England; not fencing for a place in the Essex side.'

The spinners were clapped from the field by their colleagues and the crowd stood to them. This was one of the great victories of county cricket, and this was the stuff of champions.

Essex now faced a period of inactivity until the Benson and Hedges final, inactivity punctuated only by defeat in the Sunday League game at Luton where Northamptonshire were easy winners, but where Denness, playing because Gooch was on Test duty, was Essex top scorer with 44.

CHAPTER 10

A Day to Remember–The Benson and Hedges Final

The eve of the Benson and Hedges final was spent in practice and consultation, but generally with the emphasis on relaxation. Some of the side had decided to stay in London on the Friday evening, others, like Graham Gooch, who live closer to London, spent Friday at home.

There had been some tension over a question of new blazers, and, perhaps, a committee unused to success at the highest level could have made better social arrangements for the final than they did, but experience is a teacher.

Surrey had had several misfortunes with injury and the composition of their side for Lord's would not be known until the morning of the match. Essex had no injury problems, but they, too, delayed announcing their side until the Saturday morning.

It surprised few people when Denness was named as Gooch's opening partner. Lilley was twelfth man and Acfield suffered the fate of many good spinners in limited overs cricket; he was omitted.

The day was fine. The sun shone, but the hint of breeze kept the temperature down.

Lord's on a cup-final day is a place of excitement with a glorious sense of occasion, and as the blue, gold and red favours dominated, there was a feeling that this was to be Essex's day.

The crowd gathered happily, bubbling in anticipation. Inside the ground Essex members, Roy Pawsey prominent, had taken over as unofficial stewards, shepherding those Essex supporters with unreserved seats into pockets of support.

The circuit of the ground before the match begins is a neces-sary part of a day at Lord's. It is then that one renews acquain-tance with so many friends met through cricket. One significant fact discovered during the walk round on Saturday, 21 July was that by 10.30 a.m. all Essex rosettes had been sold at the stalls by the Grace Gates.

The surprise announcement came that Surrey had won the toss, but had asked Essex to bat. The wicket looked beautiful and it was difficult to understand Roger Knight's decision. He reasoned that his bowling was weakened through injury and he wished to play to his strength which he saw as his batmen's ability to reach a target. Essex welcomed the chance to bat first.

Mike Denness said later that he had played at Lord's many times, for England, and for Kent in Gillette and Benson and Hedges finals, but never had been greeted by such a roar as the one which met him and Gooch as they came down the steps of the pavilion to open the Essex innings. Even the neutrals were willing an Essex victory.

The roar covered the ground again when Denness drove graciously through the off-side field for the first boundary of the match. In the first three overs he and Gooch scored 21 runs and though Roger Knight's accuracy stemmed the flow a little, the Lord's crowd continued to be thrilled by shots of power and beauty.

Gooch had cut Jackman square, flicked Wilson off his toes to the fine leg boundary and now drove Knight through mid-wicket off the back foot, so that runs were coming at four an over. With 50 only two runs away and Wilson bowling from the pavilion end, his run starting almost from the Long Room itself, Denness drove a little lazily and Smith took a comfortable catch at cover. It was the eleventh over of the match. Colin Cowdrey wrote afterwards that he had never seen Denness bat better.

When a boy the present writer once sat close to the legendary R.H. Twining as he waited to bat. The great man shook with nerves, his bat trembling as if with ague, and yet, when he went to the wicket, he was within minutes batting with ease and elegance, the consummation of many a summer. Ken McEwan is of this category. For Winston Smith in *1984* rats were the ultimate horror; for Ken McEwan one feels that the opening of the door to 'Room 101' would reveal a flight of pavilion steps leading to the wicket, down which he is thrust with a bat in his hand.

It is, perhaps, this frailty and humility which is the very essence of his attractiveness as person and player. In his customary frenetic opening, he slashed twice at Wilson without making contact.

Knight had settled into a steady rhythm and when Intikhab joined the attack we saw some of the best bowling of the day. But McEwan was now in touch and Gooch was solid, purposeful aggression. It was Graham who decided to break the shackles that Knight was trying to impose and he moved down the wicket and hit the Surrey captain high to the nursery end sight screen for six. The initiative now passed completely to Essex as McEwan cover drove two fours, hooked a third and pulled a fourth. They were blows of savage ferocity and Pocock, in particular, suffered mercilessly.

Gooch reached 50, but McEwan soon overtook him — his 50 coming off only 68 balls. At lunch 37 overs had been bowled and Essex were 166 for 1.

The wine corks popped. The chicken, or the salmon, or the cheese, or simply the pork pie and crisps, tasted good, but nothing could rival the champagne we had sipped in those two hours before lunch. Essex were in sight of their first-ever title and it was being accomplished in the grandest manner possible.

Shortly after lunch, with only 6 more runs scored, McEwan sliced a ball from Wilson to Richards behind the wicket. He had batted for 96 minutes during which time he had hit 10 fours in his 72, scored off 99 balls. The stand between McEwan and Gooch had realised 124, a record stand for a Benson and Hedges final and a lasting joy to all those who saw it.

Whatever thoughts Surrey may have nurtured of breakthrough or containment were quickly dispelled by Fletcher. There is always the feeling for a player who, after a long and distinguished career, finds himself in a cup final for the first time. It is a chance that may never come again. Fletcher had worked all his cricket life for a day like this and he was determined to stamp his own mark upon the game.

The Surrey fielding began to wilt. One over from Jackman, sadly unfit for such a contest as this, cost 17 runs. Fletcher smote one off-drive off the back foot of such power that those on the grass hardly had time to scatter before the ball crashed among them.

In trying to give himself room to force a ball from Knight to the off-side tavern boundary, Fletcher overbalanced and was bowled. He had been at the wicket for little over half an hour and had faced only 30 balls from which he had scored 34 runs. It was a magnificent miniature.

Throughout this time we had been savouring one of the very greatest innings that has ever been played in limited-over cricket; the power, the consolidation, the range of shots and the personality, all were there. Gooch's century, the first ever recorded in a Benson and Hedges final, was three hours of majesty. As Wilson moved in from his mammoth run Gooch ambled forward and flicked the ball off his toes into the Mound Stand. Almost passively he repeated the shot onto the roof of the stand; then he pulled viciously for 4, the crowd diving for safety as the ball parted them.

Hardie was out when going for a big hit and then with the score at 276 in the 53rd over Gooch swung inelegantly at Wilson and was bowled. He had scored 120, including three 6's and eleven 4's.

When a wicket falls there is an instinctive cry from the gathering and then the murmur of acclaim. As Gooch left the wicket the applause began and the crowd rose as one. In his autobiography Sir Pelham Warner wrote of his beloved Lord's 'Even now, after so many years, I feel something of a thrill as I walk down St John's Wood Road, and my heart, maybe, beats a shade faster as I enter the ground.' Sir Pelham would have thrilled with us at the Benson and Hedges final, for Gooch had played the innings of his life and he had played it at Lord's where all great innings should be played.

The Essex innings ended with Turner and Pont, who had struck some fine blows, running a bye to the wicket-keeper. It brought the total to 290 for 6, a record for the Benson and Hedges final.

Knight had considered his batting to be his strength, and Butcher and Lynch began with some confidence. Alan Butcher was in fine form at this time, and he was later to gain international recognition. With the score at 21, however, and Butcher on 13, Lever produced the ball of the match. It cut back at the left hander, took the inside edge, and there was Smith throwing the ball into the air with joy.

Lynch had been preferred to the more sedate Clinton, but there was an air of over-impatience about the young man from Guyana. East was now operating from the Nursery End and Lynch drove at him fretfully. McEwan moved in from deepish mid-off and judged the catch perfectly.

Knight joined Howarth and now we witnessed a crucial stand. Without ever displaying quite the panache of the Essex batting, they still contrived to put Surrey on a footing from which victory was possible. After 30 overs Surrey were ahead of Essex at the same juncture, but, respectfully, the batting was never of the same dominant and threatening quality.

The Essex fielding was of its usual very high standard, and here, perhaps, one can reflect on such a player as John Lever. He was the most successful bowler in England in 1979; how does one measure his outstanding contribution in the field?

It is not so difficult for Surrey to measure the contribution that Roger Knight's captaincy and Mickey Stewart's management have brought to the organisation of a county that had finished 1978 limping badly. Knight's contribution was manifest on the field as he and Howarth added 91 in 18 overs. Pont, in particular, was coming in for some punishment, but it was he, and Neil Smith, who broke the stand. Knight drove hard at Pont, but the ball flew off the edge high to Smith's right and the wicket-keeper took a magnificent acrobatic catch which was reminiscent of Bairstow's catching of Gooch in the semi-final. Smith well deserved the hugs of his colleagues.

David Smith immediately began to hit the ball hard and Howarth was always looking for runs. For once Turner erred in direction and the New Zealander took 14 from the over. Fletcher was calming and cajoling his side; his field placings were shrewd, his manipulation of his bowlers intelligent.

Lever was brought back, this time at the Nursery End. The object of the change was to dismiss Howarth. Lever dropped one a little short. Howarth went for the hook and Mike Denness, unbelievably, dropped a not too difficult catch at fine leg. Although there were over 100 runs needed to win, there were 18 overs left and 7 wickets in hand, and a Surrey win was possible as long as Howarth remained.

Howarth had not learned from his escape against Lever and struck out wildly at Pont. He pulled a short ball first bounce into the crowd, but it was a dangerous shot, just eluding two fielders and nearly bringing disaster. Rather unwisely he was going for the six when the four would have sufficed. Again Pont dropped a little short. Again Howarth swung wildly. The ball soared into the air and there was Fletcher, in closer at mid-on to save the single, underneath it. The ball spiralled and dropped agonisingly slowly. The captain clutched it lovingly to his chest. It was not a difficult catch, but no-one envied Fletcher as he waited for the ball to come down, particularly as his career had been spent catching sharp chances off the edge of the bat and not skiers. His team rushed to congratulate him and this, surely, was the decisive wicket.

One could not help but feel that the experienced Roope was too low at number six, but still at 205 for 5 in the 42nd over, Surrey were ahead of Essex at the same point in their innings. It would be true to say, however, without any intentional detriment to the Surrey batting, that it never quite matched the batting of Essex in class or in the sense of the power to come.

The ambitious Smith was bowled by Phillip and a chink in

the Surrey batting armour was now exposed. Intikhab hit the West Indian pace bowler high to long on where Keith Pont took a catch to rival the one held by Mike Brearley in the Prudential World Cup Final. Immediately the limping Jackman was beaten by the accuracy and flight of East.

Turner, compensating for the earlier lapse in direction, had bowled a vital maiden to Roope; now he beat Richards' forward push to scatter his stumps. In the course of his final spell, Turner's calf muscles were cramping with accumulated tension.

On the same ground several years previously he had said in one of those moments of despair that come to all sportsmen 'I don't know where the next wicket or the next run is coming from.' But he had fought through that bad patch with the tenacity with which he always fought to become the Wetherall Award winner as the best all-rounder in English cricket in 1974. Now he and his companions stood close to their greatest team success, the reward for the seasons of whole-hearted endeavour.

Roope had hit one majestic six into the Mound Stand and with him and Pocock together 44 were needed in 5 overs. Whatever ambitions still lurked in Surrey breasts were ended when 'Nobby' Phillip claimed his third victim, Pocock comprehensively bowled. Now the Essex supporters bubbled in expectation.

Lever bowling to Wilson from the Nursery End. Wilson pushes forward and Lever punches the air as the stumps are knocked askew. Then the players pelt for the pavilion as the cheering begins and everyone is on his feet clapping.

An inspired piece of casting by the Benson and Hedges organisation had Trevor Bailey as match adjudicator. Rightly he made no attempt whatever to disguise his joy, not only in the achievement, but in the manner of achievement. He paid a special tribute to Keith Fletcher, and there were many who were thinking, too, of Brian Taylor, Doug Insole, Tom Pearce and Trevor himself. There was never any doubt that the gold award would go to Gooch; his was an innings to warm us through the long winters.

The last word should be with the supporters. Roger Edson and Pat Hodges had prepared their day with care. It was to be a family day. They sported their straw hats with their Essex colours and they drank to success.

'Tired, but extremely happy, we all agreed that this had been a day to remember, but of all the memories we have of this day, none will stand out more than that of the middle-aged man who came over to us after the match with tears in his eyes and quite unashamedly told us that he had been crying. "After 103 years," he said, "we have at last won something."

And the greatest thing was, we all felt part of it.'

CHAPTER 11

The Surge on the Title

We all celebrated in our different ways and at different places. Pat, Roger and others felt that any celebration had to be held within the County boundaries. Some consoled their Surrey friends while enjoying the hospitality of Frank and Sheila at The Cricketer's Club. The players themselves had arranged their own social evening with their wives and girl friends at The Sportsman's Club, Tottenham Court Road.

It was a sober evening, and in many ways subdued. As Fletcher said later, the Benson and Hedges Cup was the icing on the cake; the Schweppes County Championship was the realisation of a dream. And there was still a long way to go in the championship.

On the Sunday evening, the day after the final, more than one Essex player remarked ruefully, 'In no way should a team which has been involved in the Benson and Hedges final be asked to play a John Player League game the next day.'

Having reached intoxicating heights at Lord's on the Saturday, the players were bound to feel a sense of deflation on the Sunday. The game at Colchester where Yorkshire were the visitors was good humoured and the crowd welcomed the heroes rapturously, but the concern of Essex now was to prepare themselves for the visit to Bournemouth on the Wednesday.

In any season certain matches are seen to have a richer significance in the overall pattern of the year than others. We have already suggested that the matches against Glamorgan at Ilford, Derbyshire at Chelmsford and Nottinghamshire at Southend played a crucial part in the destiny of the championship pennant. In talking to Essex players at the end of the season, however, one was struck by the consistency with which they selected the game against Hampshire at Bournemouth as their most exhilarating performance and the one which they felt stamped them as champions.

Hampshire had been early-season pace-makers, but few felt that they possessed the all-round quality needed to sustain a challenge in any of the competitions. Greenidge, obviously, was a world-class player; Marshall had had an impressive first season; and the persevering Keith Stevenson had enjoyed a splendid year, but there was something of a void in the side in both spin bowling and middle-order batting. No contest against them was easy, however.

Hampshire batted first on a true pitch, evenly paced. The only encouragement to the bowlers was the somewhat humid atmosphere — of this the Essex bowlers were to take full advantage. A crowd of close on three thousand had gathered to watch the new Benson and Hedges cup winners and they were given full value for money.

Greenidge, though handicapped by a leg injury, began in his usual brisk manner. He scored all of the first 16 runs. The score had progressed to 40 without qualms for Hampshire supporters when Greenidge aimed to drive at Lever, bowling from the town end, and gave the faintest of deflections to Smith behind the wicket.

Turner had replaced Phillip and he hustled one past Rice to take middle and off; then he had David Turner superbly caught at slip by McEvoy, and Hampshire were 48 for 3.

Jesty and Rock hung on determinedly, but Jesty drove loosely at Lever and McEvoy held his second catch, this time at cover. Cowley went lbw to the first ball of Lever's next over, and with the field now grouped about the bat like lions waiting for their prey (sometimes there were five in the slips), Essex took lunch in ravenous mood.

In the third over after lunch Lever bowled the resolute Rock and Taylor gave the exuberant Smith his second catch. Hampshire stood at 88 for 7 on a good wicket and before three o'clock on the first afternoon Essex had scented victory.

Some brave defence from Bob Stephenson saw Hampshire to 128, but they were all out in the 54th over so giving Essex 146 overs in which to build a decisive advantage.

Once more John Lever had been the dominant force. He had bowled all but 4 of the 27 overs bowled from the town end, demonstrating not only his control, but also his intelligent variety and consistent hostility. His ability to swing the ball, his imagination and his stamina had been rewarded with yet another set of outstanding figures — 23 overs, 7 maidens, 40 runs, 7 wickets.

Marshall bowled with great fire for Hampshire and troubled McEvoy, substituting for the injured Denness, but it was Mike Taylor who dismissed the young opener.

Gooch was again in splendid form. This was the vein of gold and once more he and McEwan cut, drove and pulled an opposing attack to pieces. The sun seemed to shine the brighter when they were batting.

Returning in the last hour, Marshall dismissed them both, but Essex finished the day 23 runs ahead with 7 wickets in hand. Their cricket radiated with belief in their own success.

Gooch's 70 was, in fact, his last significant innings of the summer for Essex. It contained 10 fours and was as exciting as it was entertaining and technically accomplished, brilliant with power, variety of shots and elegance. 1979 saw Graham Gooch emerge as one of the most exciting batsmen of his generation, a player of world class. He evoked eulogies from such noted critics as Arlott and Keating that could put him among the legendary names of cricket. Yet one has a reservation. So often he falls for 70 or 80 when 100, at least, is his for the taking, and this would suggest that there still needs to be a tightening of mental approach. When his mental powers become the equal of his physical powers his place in the World XI will be unquestioned.

The second day did not begin well for Essex. Extracting some life from the pitch Marshall and Stevenson bowled Hampshire back into the game. Only ten runs came in the first half an hour during which time Marshall bowled Phillip and Fletcher, both beaten for pace. Stevenson then removed Turner lbw and

Smith caught behind, and Essex were 208 for 7 and tottering.

Ray East's best contributions with the bat have invariably been made when he has come in as night watchman, but here he was coming in at number nine with the third batting bonus point still 42 runs away and the fourth batting point 50 runs beyond that. There can be few counties, however, who can enjoy the luxury that Essex enjoy of batting at number nine a man who has scored a first-class hundred (against Hampshire at Chelmsford in 1976) and who has scored over five thousand runs in first-class cricket at an average of nearly 18.

There is a stiff-limbed characteristic about East's batting and his antics which belies the quickness of his movement and the quality of his technique. At times he looks like a puppet which has broken its strings and gone berserk, but the frenzied gestures of the comedian hide an agonising desire to win, and to win for Essex.

Not only did Ray East help Brian Hardie to secure the third batting point, but he was still there when the fourth was obtained. In all they were together for less than an hour and a half. They received 24 overs and they added 114 runs.

Brian Hardie first stamped his name on the cricket public in May, 1974. Essex were playing Hampshire at Chelmsford and in the second innings he batted for two hours and twenty-two minutes and scored 4 runs. The 'dour' Scot made the headlines, and the record books were searched for all-time achievements in slowness of scoring. Once established, such a reputation is hard to erase and there are many, five years later, who remain blind to the several splendidly aggressive innings that Brian Hardie has played since that day.

In a sense Hardie's style emphasises rock-like qualities. His front foot is thrust exaggeratedly forward at the ball, and his high-held head seems to be inviting a blow. But the man has strength in the shoulder and power in the shot and he hits the ball very hard, and very often. Over and above his ability to hit the ball is his ability to survive when others are failing.

East played some fine shots and one or two of his own invention, including hooking Jesty for 4 when pivoting like a ballerina. Perhaps intoxicated by the thoughts of an approaching fifty, East finally became Jesty's only victim when he drove the medium pacer high to long-on into the waiting hands of Rock.

The initiative, though briefly in the morning it may have passed to Hampshire, was now positively with Essex. Lever stayed put while 18 were added and then David Acfield joined Brian Hardie.

There is nothing so destructive to the morale of a side than when the opponents make a last wicket stand of substance. Acfield likes batting, and the longer Brian Hardie was at the wicket the more formidable an adversary he became. In the end David Acfield fell to Keith Stevenson and Essex were all out for 380. The last three wickets had added 172 runs. This was batting in depth. This is what the Essex players mean when they say that everyone in the side is capable of contributing something, so that if one or two fall, there is always someone to step into the breach.

Hardie finished with 146 not out. It was a confident and utterly responsible innings, combining firm defence with bold aggression and at every stage shaped to the needs of the state of the game.

As if to prove that he was only human, Hardie missed Greenidge before he had scored when Hampshire began their second innings, 252 in arrears. It was a sharp chance at bat-pad, but as Hardie is now unquestionably the best fielder in the country in this position, it was a chance that he would generally have held.

Greenidge's ankle injury still handicapped him and he found running between the wickets difficult, but as he contented himself mostly with boundaries he was able to surmount the problem.

Greenidge and Rice put on 117 for the first wicket and once more Hampshire seemed to be clawing their way back into the game. Fletcher then turned to spin for the first time in the match and almost immediately Ray East took the vital wicket of Gordon Greenidge. In East's third over Greenidge went for the sweep, missed and was lbw. Then Acfield had Rice caught by Brian Hardie at 'Boot Hill', the ball turning sufficently to take the inside edge onto the pad before Hardie snapped it up. Jesty was the next to go when he played a shot suggesting mental aberration and was bowled by Acfield, and when Rock was deceived by East's quicker ball and bowled, Hampshire had lost 4 wickets for 18 runs in just over twenty minutes. Now it was the Essex spinners who were doing the damage.

Hampshire finished the day at 143 for 4. They still needed 109 to avoid an innings defeat and on the Friday morning *The Guardian* carried the headline 'Essex head for their first championship.' There was still a little way to go yet, though.

For the third day the sun shone vigorously and Essex sprinted onto the field in eager anticipation of finishing the job quickly.

Bob Stephenson, who had come in as night watchman, held out doggedly for ten minutes until he pushed forward at Acfield and Brian Hardie snapped up the catch at bat-pad. Acfield was now turning the ball appreciably and Cowley's vigil was ended when he edged the off-spinner to Neil Smith.

Turner and Taylor showed some resistance, but Fletcher now thought the time right to bring East into the attack again and he replaced Lever who had had a 45-minute spell. The move proved successful for Turner, who was batting low in the order because he was suffering from a virus infection, pushed forward blindly at East and Smith took another catch.

In the next over Taylor scooped Acfield to square-leg where East, 'resting' in between overs, accepted the gentle catch.   .

Bailey, who was playing in his first Championship match, now joined Marshall and held up Essex longer than was expected. Marshall survived a stumping chance and when Norbert Phillip was brought on he dealt with him rather severely, but it was a passing phase. Marshall changed his mind in the middle of his shot when attempting to drive East through mid-wicket and McEvoy took his third catch of the game, each held in a different fielding position.

Bailey hit another boundary, but in the last over before lunch he edged Phillip to Neil Smith and Essex had won by an innings and 33 runs with two sessions of play to spare.

'Essex surge on title' announced the *Daily Telegraph,* and, in truth, there seemed little now that could stop them. The spirit of the side was unquenchable. They believed they would win and this lessened stress or tension. They oozed success and they had now nine victories and a lead of 69 points in the Schweppes County Championship to prove that their confidence was justified.

Even Keith Fletcher, so apprehensive of admitting that the Championship was almost assured, was now seen to be smiling with conviction, but as he said later 'The most difficult thing was to keep the team motivated, to make them realise that it was not all over, that there was still over a month of the season to go.'

Colchester week is renowned for its eccentricity; one year the ground was flooded and all the chairs were afloat; another year snow stopped play. 1979 was to provide a further talking point for cricket historians.

The first game of the Colchester week, Essex v. Gloucestershire, began on Saturday, 28 July at 11.00 a.m. At close of play, 6.30 p.m., the scores were Gloucestershire 92 and 66 for 1, Essex 170; 328 runs had been scored in the day and 21 wickets had fallen.

The pitch looked perfect and Procter had no hesitation in batting when he won the toss. The reason for the batting debacle which followed was that groundsman Eddie Neath had rolled the wicket when it was wet and had produced a bowler's paradise. It was described as an 'experimental wicket', but you do not play Championship matches on 'experimental' wickets. The key to the way in which the wicket behaved was that it had been too liberally watered and was, in fact, far too wet when it was rolled. The result was that before lunch on the first day David Acfield could pitch a ball outside off stump which shot past Neil Smith down the leg side.

It was a day of bewildering statistics. Having reached 19 without loss, Gloucestershire lost three wickets for 1 run. Their last five wickets went down while 18 runs were scored. Andy Stovold scored 47 and batted quite splendidly. While all about him was trauma, he played as if there was nothing untoward about the wicket. He finally became one of Ray East's two victims, both obtained in collaboration with Neil Smith.

John Lever was the arch-destroyer as he destroyed the middle-order batting. He captured the wickets of Zaheer, Hignell, Procter and Bainbridge at a personal cost of 37 runs. Lever bowled only one spell of ten overs and he was greatly indebted once more to some magnificent close catching.

Essex supporters rubbed their hands gleefully and Gloucester-shire were tumbled out for 92 in 36 overs. They believed that they were witnessing one more instalment in the continuing saga of the Essex slaughter of the innocents. When Gooch, Denness and Fletcher were all back in the pavilion with only 7 runs scored it was a little difficult to discern who were the innocents and who were the slaughterers. When McEwan, Hardie and Smith were all dismissed with the score at 37 the identity of the slaughterers seemed to have been most positively determined.

'Cometh the hour, cometh the man,' said the late, and much lamented, Eddie Paynter when he went out to bat against Australia at The Oval in 1938 with the England score at 546 for 3. 'Just the man for a crisis.'

37 for 6. Phillip and Turner both on nought. These two bats-men know only one way to answer a challenge. They attacked the bowling.

Essex had won the Benson and Hedges Cup because, in the end, they had batted better, bowled better and, most certainly, fielded better than Surrey. The same simple explanation can be given for Essex beating Gloucestershire at Colchester though the wicket was at its most spiteful on the Saturday afternoon when Phillip, Turner, East, Lever and Acfield were batting.

In the first place Turner and Phillip refused to be inhibited and batted boldly. Their athleticism, their running between the wickets were a joy to behold. Secondly they benefitted from the fact that Gloucestershire failed to hold snicks, difficult half chances, which Essex fielders would have taken. Gooch, Denness and Fletcher all held catches which were as difficult as anything that Gloucestershire missed. Thirdly the Gloucestershire attack could never maintain the same relentless accuracy that the Essex bowlers had done. The simplicity of winning is that you do everything better than your opponents.

Phillip and Turner had been confronted with humiliation. Their reply was to bat Essex into the lead in the most thrilling manner possible. They had added 69 effervescent runs in 16 overs when Turner, for once forsaking aggression, pushed forward at the left-armed spin of Childs and was caught by Sadiq in the gully. He had made 35, and only Stovold and Phillip scored more in the first innings.

Essex were not done yet. East and Phillip added 26 before East was bowled by Childs for 15. Stovold had been the only Gloucestershire player to reach double figures.

Lever and Phillip added another 16 for the ninth wicket and then there was Acfield again, 5 not out, seeing Essex, incredibly, to a batting bonus point and joining Norbert Phillip in an invaluable last wicket stand of 22. The last four wickets had added 133 runs.

The last man out was Norbert Phillip. He touched Graveney to the wicket-keeper when he had made 62. His innings, which had shown marked control of shot and temperament, included 6 fours and one exciting straight six off Mike Procter who, one felt, could have bowled his off-breaks a little earlier in the Essex innings.

In the evening the wicket played better and Gloucestershire had lost Sadiq, lbw to East, before the close, but had scored 66, so reducing the Essex lead to 12.

Rain on the Sunday restricted the John Player League game to 21 overs each innings and Essex won a thrilling last over victory due to a superb knock by Keith Pont who had put on 31 in 4 overs with Stuart Turner. The England team for the Second Cornhill Test at Lord's was announced on the Sunday and it included Gooch and Lever.

The frivolities of Sunday were quickly banished when play

resumed on Monday morning and Stovold and Zaheer came out to continue the Gloucestershire innings.

In the second over of the day Zaheer swung at Turner and the skied catch was taken by Neil Smith. It could not have been a better start to the day, the most feared batsman had been dismissed and Gloucestershire had still not wiped out the first innings arrears. The wicket was giving assistance to the bowlers though the turn was slow and less eccentric than on Sunday.

Hignell and Stovold batted with great resolution and put on 67 before Stovold, who had once more played a most impressive innings, fell to a ball from Lever which the bowler held back a little. Stovold was taken easily at mid-off by Acfield.

It was Acfield who now took over the leading role. He was now operating from the end which had previously been given to Ray East and he soon had Procter beautifully caught at short-leg by Fletcher for nought. In his next over Bainbridge was caught bat-pad and Partridge at second slip by Fletcher again without scoring. When Hignell was out, another Hardie-Acfield bat-pad victim, the off-spinner had taken 4 wickets in 15 balls and Gloucestershire had gone from 140 for 3 to 145 for 7.

David Graveney defended with much good sense and the last three wickets added 60 runs, the innings coming to an end at about four o'clock. David Acfield took the six middle wickets of the innings at a cost of 56 runs. He had bowled 40 overs, 15 of them maidens. It was the third consecutive match in which Acfield had taken five wickets in an innings.

Had David Acfield played his cricket in the 1930s he would have grabbed his hundred wickets a season, commanded a regular place in any county side and come close to international honours. He had played his cricket in the 1970s, however, an age dominated by seam bowling and limited-over cricket. He has never been sure of playing in every first-class match and in 1979 he played in only ten of Essex's 24 limited-over games. In spite of this he was able to bowl Essex to victory or to a position of strength whenever such a task was demanded of him. It is correct to say that Essex would not have won the Championship without Lever or without McEwan or without Gooch or ... It is equally true to say that they would never had won it without the efforts of David Acfield as bowler, and batsman, in the month of July.

Essex needed 128 for victory when they began their second innings. They lost both Gooch and McEwan for 28 and things did not look too good. Denness was dropped twice, but he and Fletcher were masters of spin and too good for the Gloucestershire attack. Denness went at 89 and Fletcher at 108. Both Hardie and Phillip were out with the score on 119, but Essex were safe now and with the extra half an hour claimed they took their tenth win of the Championship on the second day. Inevitably they finished with a flourish, Turner hitting Graveney over mid-on for 6.

The month of July ended with Graham and Brenda Gooch pictured in the *Daily Mirror*. Essex stars were shining everywhere. Kent, or rather Derek Underwood, had routed Nottinghamshire and the Essex lead in the Schweppes County Championship was 82 points.

What a marvellous month it had been; the Benson and Hedges Cup had been won in glorious fashion and three County Championship victories had all but destroyed those challenging Essex for the title.

What we did not know at the end of July was that the 207 points that Essex had accumulated were already enough to win them the Championship. Had we known that no other county would reach that total by the end of the season, we would have found the first weeks of August less agonising.

CHAPTER 12

The Spectre of August Failure

In the past, whenever Essex had seemed to be moving towards the winning of the County Championship or, more recently, the John Player League, the pessimists had nodded their heads knowingly and said, 'Wait until August.' And they had been proved right time and again.

The last phase of the season had always seen a collapse in the fortunes of Essex. Both physically and mentally the team had faded. It was as if some psychological barrier erected itself which Essex teams, generation after generation, were incapable of scaling. For Essex, August was like the Ides of March for Julius Caesar; it was the end of ambition.

August, 1979, presented Essex with a strange fixture list in their last lap of the Championship race. They met Middlesex at Colchester, then travelled to Worcester. As the Gillette Cup Quarter Finals were scheduled for Wednesday the eighth, and Essex met India on the following Saturday and had no game on Wednesday, 15 August, they would not then play a Schweppes County Championship game until they went to Northampton on Saturday, 18 August. Much of their time would be spent in sitting and seeing how their rivals fared.

A delayed start at Colchester against Middlesex only put off the misery that awaited Essex. Keith Fletcher won the toss and decided to bat, and within half an hour he was one of the three batsmen out with only nine runs scored. Wayne Daniel and Mike Selvey, gaining help from the wicket, bowled Essex out in 38.2 over for 106, of which Brian Hardie made 41.

Middlesex batted solidly in reply and a little stodgily. It was the stodginess which prompted Keith Fletcher to give his leg-breaks another airing. He bowled 15.3 overs and took 5 wickets for 41, a career-best bowling performance. His wickets included top scorer Clive Radley and Fred Titmus who was making a surprise re-appearance in the Middlesex side. It is interesting to note that Fletcher finished the season with nine wickets at a cost of 14.88 runs each. One more wicket would have placed him second in the first-class averages for the country.

As Essex finished Thursday evening at 13 for 2 there seemed little hope of saving the game. Fletcher and Pont hit fifties on the Friday and, with a storm circling Colchester, it seemed possible that Essex might escape defeat. It was not to be. Titmus dismissed Fletcher, Featherstone took four wickets and Gatting and Smith hit off the runs needed for victory in just over seven overs; and then the rains came.

It was the first defeat Essex had suffered in the Schweppes County Championship since they had lost to Surrey at The Oval in May of the previous year. The defeat had little bearing on the Championship as, though Essex had picked up only three points in the game with Middlesex, Nottinghamshire had gained only one more in their draw at Worcester. The Championship table remained almost totally unaffected.

The Essex players shrugged their shoulders at the defeat by Middlesex. They felt that they had the worst of all the luck that was going, particularly with regard to the wicket, and they felt that fate, rather than inadequacies on their own part, was the main contributor to their defeat. They did not hold the same philosophical opinion about what happened at Worcester.

Early on Tuesday morning Essex were beaten by an innings and 22 runs. Facing 353 for 9, they had made 185 and 146. They made no excuses about this one.

'We were terrible. They batted better, bowled better and fielded better than we did. They stuffed us out of sight.'

Worcestershire took 20 points, Essex 5, and Worcestershire now moved into second place in the table, 71 points behind Essex, but with a game in hand.

Worcestershire used up their game in hand when they met
Kent at Canterbury. They bowled Kent out for 160, but failed
to gain maximum batting points when, in spite of a magnificent
innings of 170 from Younis Ahmed, they were all out for 286
in 102.2 overs. Nevertheless, Worcestershire seemed to be heading
for victory when Kent were 64 for 3 in the second innings, Woolmer, Rowe and Asif Iqbal being out. Alan Ealham and Chris
Tavare then put on 251 for Kent's fourth wicket and the match
ended in a draw. Worcestershire had to be content with 7 points.
It must be one of the few occasions in cricket history when Essex
supporters were shouting for Kent. It meant that with three top
sides in the Schweppes County Championship each having five
games left to play, Essex led by 64 points.

Meanwhile the Essex hangover continued. They batted first
against the Indians at Chelmsford and were soon enduring further
nightmares. Graham Gooch hung out his bat to a ball outside
the off-stump from Kapil Dev and guided a catch to Gavaskar.
As if to show he could do the same thing, Denness touched
Amarnath to the wicket-keeper. The indiscretions continued
and Essex went to 55 for 7.

Without any disrespect to the Indian tourists, many of the
Essex players were finding it hard to give the match their full
concentration, a point which Turner seemed to be making when
he swung wildly and was bowled for nought. So much effort,
emotional and physical, had gone into winning the Benson and
Hedges Cup and into placing one hand firmly upon the Championship shield, that it was difficult to treat too seriously a game
which, in spite of the generous sponsorship of Holt's Products,
was almost exclusively social in importance.

Keith Fletcher was concerned, however, that his side should
recover its batting composure of July, and he played an innings
which shamed his colleagues. He batted for more than 60 overs
before he finally became Chandrasekhar's fourth victim when
he was bowled in trying to cut. He had made 64. He and Neil
Smith, who once more swung his bat to good effect, put on 90
for the eighth wicket. Smith was another Chandrasekhar victim,

caught close in when four short of his 50.

The last three wickets fell whilst only one run was scored and the Essex total finished at 146. One of the beauties of the day was the bowling of Bedi. His control of flight, intelligent in variety, constantly probing at the batsman, had brought him the wickets of McEwan and Phillip at a cost of 19 runs. He had bowled 22 overs of artistry and it was a little sad to think that we were probably seeing this great cricketer, and character, in Essex for the last time.

The Essex score was meagre, but when Norbert Phillip took the wickets of Gavaskar, Chauhan and Vengsarkar with only 19 runs on the board, it began to look better. Yashpal Sharma and Mohinder Amarnath then brought some sanity back to the art of batting, and on the Sunday Sharma completed a very good hundred.

There had been little urgency about the cricket and Sunday was a sedate and lazy day. India declared with a lead of 65, but Gooch and Denness at last gave Essex supporters something to cheer about when they quickly wiped out this lead. Gooch and Fletcher fell before the close, and with Denness and Smith at the crease, Essex finished the day on 91 for 2.

The Monday morning saw the best batting of the match and suddenly Essex seemed alive and well again. Mike Denness had played well on the Sunday and he continued his innings as if there had been no interruption. He completed an excellent 50, giving a lesson in how to play spin bowling, and was rightly angry with himself when he misread the bounce from a Chandrasekhar leg-break and steered the ball to Gavaskar in the gully.

The departure of Denness brought Ken McEwan to the wicket. His innings was to last for only 41 minutes, but during that time he hit 68. As McEwan had failed to reach 30 since his scintillating 185 against Derbyshire in June, twelve innings before, it was a knock which brought sighs of relief to the Essex camp. In one over from Venkataraghavan he hit three fours and a six. Bedi, bowling from the River Chelmer end, brought up his mid-on and mid-off, so McEwan walked down the wicket and twice hit

him into the area of the new tea stand. It was Bedi who beat
him in the end when he pushed one through a little bit quicker
and flatter. The stand with Smith had realised 82 and the York-
shireman, an aggressive bat, had been made to look a sluggard.

Hardie was out to Bedi in the same over as McEwan and so
collected a 'pair'. If a batsman has to have this experience,
Hardie chose the right match for his turn.

The departure of McEwan did not stop the Essex onslaught.
Smith was now in full cry and found a willing partner in Keith
Pont. Smith was caught at mid-off by Bedi off Chauhan for 65,
but Pont hit the same bowler for two sixes and was 40 not out
when Fletcher declared, leaving India to make 227 in three hours.

As 75 minutes had been lost at the start of the day because
of rain, this was a generous declaration, but when Gavaskar was
caught behind off Lever, a lovely catch by Smith taken low down,
the Indians settled for batting practice and a draw. Three of their
players, Vengsarkar, who had been struck on the knee while
fielding, Gaekwad, who had an upset stomach, and Kapil Dev,
who had a bad knock, were nursing ailments so the Indians'
decision was probably a wise one, if a little disappointing.

We mentioned earlier the social aspects of the game against
the tourists and it is well that we should reflect upon this for a
moment.

One of the most important components of Essex cricket is its
social vitality and the accessibility of the players. Friends from
Middlesex, for example, are often staggered to find how easy it
is to rub shoulders with, and chat to, members of the team in
the pavilions at Chelmsford, Colchester, Southend and Ilford.
The sense of involvement between player and spectator has
created a unity of purpose, a club spirit, which is second to
none.

Mike Denness has commented upon how easy he found the
transition from Kent to Essex, not only because of the wit and
humour of his new team mates, but also because of the after-
match tradition of joining members, friends or hosts in a drink.

The Essex grounds are ringed with tents, Chelmsford has its

brick-built arbours too, where business firms entertain and watch cricket. Their support, financial and moral, is vital to the survival of the County Club.

No Essex match would be complete without the sign announcing 'Martin's the Newsagents', and Mr. Martin himself has been a great benefactor of the club. In recent years the name of Access has been equally prominent. The organisation has, at times, offered winter employment to some of the players and, like other hosts and sponsors, has always been generous to beneficiaries. On match days the Access tent is a colourful presence on the ground with its uniformed pretty girls and that supreme master of ceremonies, Stuart Curtis, dispensing bonhomie in all directions.

No game against the touring side would ever be complete without the large tent alongside the pavilion at Chelmsford where for three days Overseas Containers Limited entertain their friends which always include the touring party itself.

Some businessmen may say 'Why? Is it worth it? How much can you make out of it?'

Stanton Hughes, the O.C.L. organiser, would answer, 'How can you measure good-will? We do this once a year to say thank you to our friends. We like cricket, and we like Essex County Cricket Club, and it is our way of being happy with everybody.' Stanton and O.C.L. would be greatly missed if their tent was not in evidence at the tourists' match.

There was no day off for the players on the Tuesday after the game with India for there was a Stuart Turner benefit game to be played in Basildon. When one reads enviously of the large sums of money that are raised for beneficiaries to-day, one should also reflect on the work and effort that has been put in by so many people. The beneficiary himself can expect to attend a minimum of three hundred functions during the year, everything from dinners to dart matches. His colleagues help him because they know he will help them, but it is very exhausting. As one cricketer remarked, 'Benefit year would be all right if you didn't have to play cricket as well.' Accepting that statement, the performances of Turner and East in their respective benefit seasons have been nothing short of phenomenal.

There was some rest for most people over the next three days as rain swept the country, curtailing cricket everywhere, including the Third Cornhill Test at Headingley. Lever had once more been made twelfth man, Willis, who took 21 first-class wickets at 33.28 runs each during the whole of the season compared to Lever's 106 at 17.30, was preferred. Though sorry for J.K., Essex supporters were not too disappointed from the County's point of view as it meant that their opening bowler would be available for the game at Northampton on the Saturday.

Essex eyes were far more firmly fixed on Cheltenham than on Headingley. The news was good for Essex, if not for Worcestershire. With Sadiq Mohammad hitting his seventh century of the season and Zaheer and Hignell also among the runs, Gloucestershire passed three hundred for the loss of 8 wickets. Worcestershire finished the second day at 142 for 9, still needing 17 to avoid the follow-on. It rained on the Friday and no more play was possible so that Worcestershire had to be content with only three points though, in the circumstances, they could not have hoped for more than four even if the weather had stayed fine.

So, on the evening of Friday, 17 August, Essex led the table by 61 points from Worcestershire who had played one game more. It meant that Essex travelled to Northampton knowing that the maximum 20 points would give them the Schweppes County Championship for the first time in their 103-year history.

CHAPTER 13

The Last Hurdle

On reflection it is hard to understand now why we were all so apprehensive. Did we really believe that Worcestershire would take a maximum 80 points from 4 games and that Essex would not manage to pick up 20 points from 5 games? The weather was uncertain, for sure, but the real cause of anxiety was that we had waited 103 years for the most coveted of cricket's prizes, and now that it was almost within our grasp, we found it difficult to believe that it would at last be ours.

There was some practical and sensible team selection for the game at Northampton. Gooch was in the England side at Headingley so a substitute had to be found to open with Denness. Previously, when Gooch had been with the England team, McEvoy or Lilley had come into the side. Denness, McEwan, Fletcher, Hardie, Turner, Phillip, Smith, East and Lever had held regular places in the side, and depending upon the game and the wicket, Pont or Acfield had filled the last spot. At Northampton it was decided to depend upon experience, a decision which had proved most rewarding in the Benson and Hedges final. At Northampton, Brian Hardie reverted to his original position as opening batsman and both Pont and Acfield played. Solidity, panache, variety were the Essex ingredients for the vital encounter.

Northamptonshire had run into good form late in the season, form which was to take them to the final of the Gillette Cup. This form could not sustain them against the opening attack of Lever and Phillip and they were soon reeling at 9 for 3. Larkins had been lbw in Lever's first over and then Norbert Phillip had bowled the most promising Richard Williams and, most

importantly, had the exciting Allan Lamb caught at bat-pad by
Brian Hardie for 2.

Cook and Willey batted with sense and aggression, but Stuart
Turner had Geoff Cook lbw and bowled Jim Yardley for 1.
Northamptonshire were now 83 for 5 and Essex spirits were high.

Peter Willey hit the ball with tremendous relish and though
of the remaining batsmen only Jim Watts with 12 was able to
reach double figures, Northamptonshire managed to get to 224.
That they passed two hundred was due entirely to Willey who
hit 131, coming in with the score at 9 for 3 and being ninth out
at 219. Willey's effort was quite magnificent and must have gone
a long way to securing him a place in the England side at The
Oval. He was out leg before to Turner, the seam bowler's fifth
victim. Turner's 5 wickets cost 70 runs and represented his best
figures of the season though he was to better them in the second
innings and then twice more before the season's end.

Denness and Hardie gave Essex a steady start and though
Hardie was out with the score at 22, McEwan was in sparkling
form and on Saturday evening the prospective champions were
82 for 1. They already had 4 points and life looked good. On
the Sunday they overwhelmed Leicestershire and things looked
even better. Monday morning brought a colder sense of reality.

There was little hint of any trouble at the start when Denness
and McEwan resumed their innings. They increased their stand
to 96 without the slightest sense of alarm and then Denness
edged Sarfraz to slip where Yardley took a comfortable catch.
McEwan had played much as he had done in his previous innings,
against India, but three runs later, with his score on 70, he was
leg before to Sarfraz.

Pont stayed with Fletcher and Essex seemed to be moving
serenely forward until Jim Griffiths was brought back on to
bowl. His first delivery found the edge of Pont's bat and Jim
Yardley took a superb slip catch.

Fletcher had been missed by Willey off the bowling of Tim
Lamb before he had scored, but he now batted with an assurance which made the tumble of wickets at the other end all the

more incomprehensible. Sarfraz, in particular, was causing much trouble and the last seven batsmen mustered only 18 runs altogether. Sarfraz returned his best championship figures of the season, 6 for 60, and when David Acfield touched a ball from Griffiths to Sharp behind the stumps Fletcher was 52 not out and Essex were out for 199, so collecting only one batting bonus point.

When Northamptonshire batted again John Lever had both Larkins and Williams lbw, but the home side passed the hundred without further loss. Turner then dismissed Cook and Willey in quick succession, but with the elegant Lamb and the stubborn Yardley engaging in a stand of fifty, the game once more swung towards Northamptonshire.

It was Norbert Phillip who broke the stand and he dismissed both Lamb, a most valuable wicket, and Yardley. In worsening light Stuart Turner had Sharp and Sarfraz lbw with successive balls, and when play ended early Northamptonshire were 174 for 8, a lead of 199, and Essex breathed again.

Rain had badly affected Worcestershire's game at Derby, but they had taken maximum bowling points and were 201 for 3, well on the way to maximum batting points, at the close on Monday.

It was Fletcher's policy not to worry about what the others were doing. He said simply that if Essex went on winning, it did not matter what anybody else did.

The last two Northamptonshire wickets proved stubborn, but Turner made his haul 5 for 56 when he bowled Tim Lamb, and Jim Griffiths finally fell to John Lever. Essex needed 229 to win, the highest score of the match.

Essex had five hours in which to get the runs. The wicket was probably at its best and Northamptonshire were handicapped when Sarfraz left the field before lunch with an injured back, but it would have taken more than Sarfraz, splendid bowler as he is, to have halted the determined Scotsmen, Hardie and Denness. Unhurriedly, they set Essex on the way to victory. The off-spin of Peter Willey restricted the scoring but they never became becalmed.

Brian Hardie reached his fifty with a three, and under ten minutes later Mike Denness also hit a three to bring up his fifty. He was out almost immediately when he chopped a Williams' off-break onto his stumps. The first wicket had realised 113.

McEwan was soon into his stride and pulled a massive six to mid-wicket, but then was given lbw, the fourteenth of the match, to Peter Willey.

There must be no panic now and Fletcher saw to it that there would be none. Gradually he and Hardie eased the Essex score nearer to the required total. Hardie now looked impregnable. At tea Essex needed 64 runs and when the final twenty overs were called they needed 30 to win.

It was a little sad that Fletcher was not there at the finish — no man has served his county better — but with the score at 210, and his at 39, he gave Jim Yardley a slip catch off Larkins. Pont joined Hardie.

Pont played as responsibly and as intelligently as he had done in the Benson and Hedges semi-final against Yorkshire and he made sure that Brian Hardie reached the century that his effort so richly deserved.

With the score on 226 for 3 and ten overs remaining, Jim Watts called up Jim Yardley for his first over of the season. It was never completed for three balls later Brian Hardie made the winning hit.

17 points had been taken from the match and all now depended on what had happened at Derby. Worcestershire had scored their three hundred runs and finally bowled out Derbyshire for 158. This meant that they needed 25 to win. Derbyshire had been bowled out in the 19th over of the last hour, and there were ten minutes remaining. Worcestershire believed that they had 4 overs in which to make the runs, but at 17 for 1 after 2 overs the umpires removed the bails. There was some anger and controversy, but of this Essex knew nothing as they waited by the radio at Northampton for the six o'clock cricket scores.

'Essex have won the Schweppes County Championship....'

Nobody heard any more. John Lever was standing with his

Sharp, lbw, b Phillip. The bowler and Smith are in unison. Benson and Hedges semi-final *(Patrick Eagar)*

The Yorkshire collapse gains momentum — Athey is bowled by the jubilant East for 1 *(Patrick Eagar)*

Above Stevenson
bowled Lever 13. Old
looks on ruefully
(Patrick Eagar)

Right David Acfield:
'He should be spinning
for England, not fencing
for a place in the Essex
side' *(Sporting Pictures
(UK) Ltd)*

Opposite above Lumb
survives Lever's attempt
to run him out. Alan
Lilley is at cover. Lumb
was to fall 8 runs later
(Patrick Eagar)

Opposite below
Bairstow does not
survive — run out by
Keith Pont's under-arm
throw. His batting,
bowling and fielding
won Pont (not in
picture) the Gold Award
(Patrick Eagar)

Right One of the greatest of innings seen in limited-over cricket. Graham Gooch drives through the covers *(Patrick Eagar)*

Jack Richards wrecks the wicket and smiles apologetically, but Gooch is to continue inflicting punishment on the Surrey bowlers *(Patrick Eagar)*

Graham Gooch shows
elegance, power and
control as he hooks
Hugh Wilson into the
Mound Stand. We
watched with a sense
of wonder
(Patrick Eagar)

Below The inelegant
end of a graceful innings.
Gooch swings at Wilson
and is bowled for 120.
Pont looks anguished.
Wilson looks relieved
(Patrick Eagar)

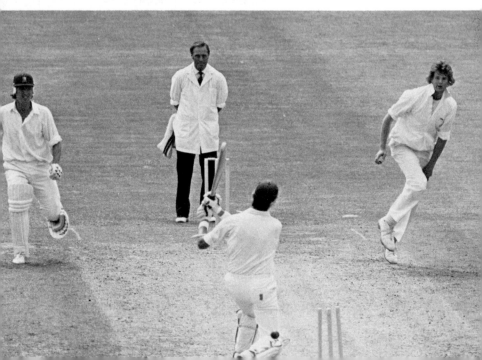

Ken McEwan hits to leg. Even a helmet cannot convince Mike Gatting that he would rather not be so close *(Sporting Pictures (UK) Ltd)*

Ray East — 'a fellow of infinite jest' *(Patrick Eagar)*

Below Brian Hardie: rock-like in defence, uninhibited in attack *(Sporting Pictures (UK) Ltd)*

Keith Fletcher: no man did more to bring glory to Essex cricket.
(Sporting Pictures (UK) Ltd)

socks in his hand. When the announcement was made he threw them in the air in celebration. One came down on Enid's head. She has kept it, washed, as her memento of that historic evening. Peter Edwards brought out the champagne and everyone sparkled. Even Enid's fruit juice, her usual drink, was laced with champagne that evening.

There were the inevitable interviews and the comments about the all-round ability of the side. Keith Fletcher summed up most people's feelings when he said, 'This is the one you want to win most. The Benson and Hedges is the cream of the cake but the championship is what matters.'

Worcestershire were not happy. The events at Derby had been the third bizarre happening in a season which had seen them roll the starting handle of the mower into the wicket at Worcester and have to follow on after declaring more than a hundred behind in a match restricted to two days. There were phone calls to Lord's and Norman Gifford had much to say about the umpires, but no-one can really believe that the events at Derby had any bearing on the destiny of the title. Essex cleared up any doubts at Chelmsford four days later.

There was a large crowd for the game against Surrey and there was a battery of photographers. The team was given a hero's welcome. The match itself provided a splendid celebration.

Gooch was uneasy at the start and batted 11 overs for 4 before being caught behind off Robin Jackman. McEwan was soon into his stride, but he was bowled by Roger Knight for 22. This brought Keith Fletcher to the crease.

Fletcher has never been noted for displays of emotion. He is a quiet and thinking cricketer who is firm in judgement and positive in his demands. Those who have been with him a long time will tell you to watch for the tilt of the cap. When he is displeased it is pushed further back on his head. He was aware that he had been the butt of criticism in the years when Essex had failed to win competitions, but now he was acclaimed for his achievement. As he walked to the wicket the crowd rose to him and clapped him all the way. He was deeply moved and, perhaps, for most of us this was the moment of realisation that Essex had indeed won the Schweppes County Championship.

Fletcher cut Jackman for four and was caught by Roope when, injudiciously, he tried to repeat the shot. It made no difference to the crowd and he was applauded all the way back to the pavilion as if he had scored a hundred. Fletcher was overcome by the occasion. The many-headed monster can be as kind as it can be cruel.

Denness and Hardie batted very well and saw Essex safely to lunch, but after Denness was out for 61 the champions faltered in mid-afternoon. Pont and Turner were out of touch and when Hardie was bowled by Pocock the 300 mark seemed a long way away.

Essex had reached 246 for 8 mainly because Norbert Phillip was connecting with his mighty swings. In full flight he is a wonderful sight, uncoiling like a spring in a way that seems unique to West Indian cricketers and the ball going high and very hard to all parts of the ground. He was finally taken one-handed on the boundary by Monty Lynch when Phillip and most of the spectators thought it was another six. The score was 267 for 9.

When the score reached 250 and the third batting point was obtained there was a mighty roar from the crowd; there could be no arguments from Worcestershire or anyone else now. Roger and Pat cut the 'championship cake' which their wives had prepared and decorated, and it was a good excuse for another celebration drink. There was more fun to come.

East and Lever are good friends. Several times when batting they have engaged in a comic double act though they seem to have difficulty in deciding who should be the straight man. With the championship won and 33 runs needed for the fourth batting point, the stage was set for their antics. Both played very straight and East, in particular, drove through the off-side in upright, classical manner. Some theatrical running between the wickets saw the score creep up and, to their credit, the Surrey fielders joined in the fun. Pat Pocock bowled the hundredth over. East, with the seriousness of the great comedian, complained to the umpire about the Surrey off-spinner's delaying tactics. Pocock could scarcely bowl for laughing and the three-hundredth run and the fourth batting point came off the last delivery of the hundred overs.

The celebrations continued on the Sunday when Middlesex were slaughtered in the John Player League match, Turner collecting a share of prize money with four wickets, and, amazingly, Essex found themselves in fifth place with a chance of prize money for finishing in the first three.

There was another good crowd on the August Bank Holiday Monday when in an uneven batting display Surrey were all out only 13 short of the Essex total. Geoff Howarth hit a fine hundred before becoming one of Turner's four victims and Graham Roope reached 61 in a style which reminded one why he had played 21 times for England.

By the close Essex were 44 for 3. East, for once, had failed as night-watchman and Gooch and McEwan had both fallen to Hugh Wilson who bowled with much more fire than he had done in the first innings.

On the last day Fletcher and Denness seemed untroubled at first, but after Fletcher was out caught at slip, seemingly playing across the line, Essex collapsed and were all out for 101.

Yet another large crowd had gathered to greet the champions and there was a sense of disappointment that Surrey had been set only 115 runs to win. The ball had moved about off the seam following early morning dew, but as the day was fine, there appeared to be no reason why the batsmen should continue to be troubled as they had been in the first session.

Lynch was caught at slip by McEwan before lunch, but Butcher and Howarth gave Essex supporters no further cause for hope as they batted comfortably into the afternoon. They both fell to Lever and the ball again seemed to be coming off the pitch at varying heights as Turner exploited the conditions to dismiss Knight and Roope. Surrey had gone from 34 for 1 to 44 for 5 in a matter of minutes and the ground was bubbling with excitement.

Clinton had been to hospital for an X-ray on a badly bruised finger, but he batted with his usual tenacity. He and Jackman guided the score to 61 when Jackman was beaten by Phillip's pace and movement. Two runs later Clinton touched Lever's away swinger to Neil Smith. It was John Lever's hundredth wicket of the season and the crowd and his team-mates gave the warmest of ovations.

If anyone should ask the question 'Will success spoil Essex? Will they still enjoy their cricket as much as they have done before?' then perhaps the answer is simply to point to John Lever. After having considerable success at international level and exciting much favourable comment on television and radio and in the press, John Lever remains one of the most unaffected of human beings. A delightful man, a charming companion, he has a kind word for everyone. Any young man starting on a career as a professional cricketer would do well to look to John Lever.

Lever also dismissed Pocock, Phillip bowled Richards, and Surrey were 78 for 9. Intikhab had battled grimly and Wilson joined him in a stubborn last-wicket stand. The tea interval was put back and after two and a half hours in the field 'Nobby' Phillip yorked Wilson and Essex had won by 15 runs. There were no doubts after this as to who were champions.

There remained one first-class game at Chelmsford, the return meeting with Northamptonshire. The ground had an aura of well-being. The sun shone and the cry 'We are the champions' really meant something.

Essex made three changes from the side that had played Surrey. Gooch and Lever were on Test duty and Pont made way for Acfield. McEvoy took Gooch's place, but he batted at number five, and in place of John Lever was Gary Sainsbury who was making his debut in first-class cricket.

The Essex bowlers struggled a little on the opening day when Wayne Larkins, fighting for a place in the side to tour Australia, hit an excellent 91 and Allan Lamb was run out for 69 which was just as well for he looked in form for more. Facing 314 for 7, Essex lost Denness early, but were 59 for 1 at the close.

Brian Hardie once more displayed his qualities when the Essex innings continued on the Thursday. McEvoy had batted better than in any other of his first-team appearances in 1979 before being lbw to Hodgson for 24 after helping Hardie in a stand of 56.

McEvoy was a little disappointed when he returned to the pavilion. 'I felt I was going really well,' he said, 'as well as at any time in the second team.'

In such circumstances a man like Mike Denness is invaluable. 'It is harder, Mike,' he said. 'You have scored over a thousand runs in the second team, but when you come into the first team you have got to concentrate harder. And when you get into the twenties you have got to concentrate harder still.' There are many lessons to be learned in becoming a professional cricketer, and they are easier to learn with people like Mike Denness and Keith Fletcher around.

Neither Phillip nor Turner stayed long and when Hardie edged Griffiths to slip Essex were 189 for 7. Hardie had batted with that combination of resolute defence and uninhibited aggression which took him to the top of the averages of Essex County Cricket Club in 1979. A sigh of disappointment went round the ground when he was out for 93.

In a sense what followed was a microcosm of the season. Few other counties would have gone much beyond 200, but Essex's sights were always set firmly on the fourth batting bonus point and until their last man had been dismissed no county could be sure of stopping them. Neil Smith and Ray East were together for 14 overs during which time they averaged six and a half runs an over. Smith was in mighty form. Five times he put the ball into the crowd and in one over from the medium-paced Alan Hodgson he hit three sixes. Graham Saville, now a national coach, but still committed to the Essex cause, was astounded by the power of Smith's shots. He almost leapt from his chair in Peter Edwards' office as Neil Smith twice hit the ball with tremendous force, and height, into the area of the car park.

Ray East was no less forceful and it was sad that once more

he just missed a well-earned fifty when he was caught by Cook off Griffiths. The stand had realised 91. David Acfield came in to play with his usual aplomb, revelling in promotion to number ten, and he was unbeaten on 12 when Neil Smith was finally caught, quite brilliantly, at square leg by Wayne Larkins. The ball was travelling very fast and Larkins took it low down. Essex had reached 303 in only 80.3 overs and Fletcher declared so as to get at Northamptonshire while they were still groggy from the Smith-East battering.

By tea Northamptonshire were battered even more badly. Cook was lbw to Sainsbury so giving the young man his first wicket in first-class cricket, and Larkins and Lamb both went to Turner in the same over. Turner was moving the ball considerably and by the close he had taken three more wickets and Northamptonshire were 135 for 8.

The Northamptonshire innings lasted only three more deliveries the next morning. Yardley turned Phillip's first ball for two, but prodded forward at the next and was caught by McEwan at slip. Jim Griffiths was bowled first ball.

Essex moved evenly to the 149 they needed for victory and it was fitting that Keith Fletcher should hit Cook for 6 to reach his own fifty and win the match. It was the thirteenth Essex win of the season.

Epilogue

There remained two matches in the Schweppes County Championship, at Leicester and Scarborough, both of which were lost. The final flourish had been at Chelmsford and Scarborough, in particular, was treated very much as a festival though Essex should still have won.

A defeat in the last John Player League game, Glamorgan at Chelmsford, denied Essex prize money in that competition, but by now the players were emotionally drained. The task had been accomplished.

Several social events were still on the calendar. There were Stuart Turner benefit matches to be played against enthusiastic village sides. Keith Fletcher played golf in a promotion for John Shepherd's benefit. Graham Gooch went off to Barbados for a short tour arranged by Duncan Fearnley in aid of Vanburn Holder's benefit. John Lever and Brian Hardie snatched a few days' holiday. John had to make some preparations for his benefit in 1980 before he left for Australia. Others thought about winter employment. Ken McEwan holidayed briefly at home in South Africa before going to Perth where he played the previous year. Norbert Phillip returned home to the West Indies.

On Friday, 12 October there was a social gathering in the Chelmsford pavilion where players, officials and members shared a drink and chatted over the summer of success, but the main celebrations were delayed until the New Year.

On Tuesday, 20 November, an Essex contingent went to Buckingham Palace. There, in the Music Room, the Lord's Taverners' Twelfth Man, His Royal Highness The Duke of

Edinburgh, presented Keith Fletcher with the trophy for winning the Schweppes County Championship. It was a great moment for Fletcher and for the others in the party. Ray East, Mike Denness, Stuart Turner, Neil Smith, David Acfield and Brian Hardie were all in attendance, and the party was completed by the President of the Club, Tom Pearce; the Chairman, 'Tiny' Waterman, the Vice-Chairman, Doug Insole; the Secretary-Manager, Peter Edwards; Physiotherapist, Ray Cole; Scorer, Clem Driver; former Captain, Brian Taylor; and the former scorer, Jack Bartlam.

After the presentation the Duke of Edinburgh chatted with the players and officials, showing particular interest in the work of Ray Cole and asking the players their plans for the winter months. Then the party moved off to be entertained by Schweppes, the sponsors of the County Championship.

Inevitably thoughts passed to the future. Steve Malone had left the club to join Hampshire, but all the other members of the staff were offered contracts. Mike Denness was persuaded to try at least one more season and Norbert Phillip was given a two-year contract as were the young players, Herbert, McEvoy, Lilley, Sainsbury, Pringle and Gladwin. The senior members of the staff were all granted three-year contracts.

The club also announced new signings in Neil Foster, a pace bowler from Colchester, and Robert Leiper, a hard-hitting left-hander from Woodford Wells. David Collier from Shropshire joined the club as assistant to Peter Edwards.

A commemorative plate and tie were announced to mark the achievements of 1979, but few who saw any part of the season will forget either the achievements or the manner in which they were accomplished.

More than any other factor, the joy with which Essex played their cricket dominated. There can be endless tactical talks and analyses of the opposition's weaknesses and strengths, but in the end the simple instruction 'Go out there and enjoy yourselves' is the only one that matters.

This sense of enjoyment permeated all that Essex did. It

generated their batting, it stimulated their bowling and, above all, it energised their fielding. Those who witnessed it will never forget the field clustered round the bat in eager anticipation when East and Acfield were bowling against Nottinghamshire at Southend, nor when John Lever was in full cry in June.

The joy spread to the welcoming of youngsters. When Gary Sainsbury had Geoff Cook leg before for his first wicket in first-class cricket mature players like Turner, Denness and East raced from all parts of the field to congratulate him.

Joy was the ingredient that gave the team its spirit and personality, and so captivated all who watched them, including the 'neutrals' who saw the Benson and Hedges final at Lord's.

Allied to the joy in their cricket Essex had technical skill and dedication in abundance. Mention has already been made of the superb fitness and application of the side. Four days after the Schweppes County Championship had been won, Essex played Surrey at Chelmsford and during the course of the first day's play, Graham Gooch took Ray East on an 'extra' training run. East came back with sweat staining his T-shirt. He flopped into a chair on the player's balcony, saying 'He's mad! He's mad!'

John Lever laughed and said, 'I warned you.' But they glowed with fitness and were eager for more, and the Championship was already won.

Though John Lever is the driving force behind, and organiser of, the fitness campaign, who can forget the dedication of Mike Denness? With years of success behind him, and in the twilight of a splendid career, Denness might have been forgiven for taking things a little easier than the others, but he spared himself not the slightest in training and practice. Like all the senior professionals at Essex he set a magnificent example to the younger players.

Denness himself is unstinting in his praise of the Essex side as the best balanced one in which he has ever played. 'At Kent,' he says, 'we geared out style to the accuracy of Derek Underwood and a wealth of medium-pace bowling. This is why I felt we were always better equipped to win the limited-over competitions. At Essex we have a side which is equipped for all conditions and all competitions.'

There is no way that one can contradict Denness's assertion. The Essex attack consists of quick right-arm, fast-medium left-arm, right-arm medium pace, slow left-arm, off-breaks and the leg-spin of Keith Fletcher, 'Not the worst leg-break bowler in the world', as Denness describes him. No other county can boast such a varied and balanced bowling array.

The batting presents an equally exciting variety: opening batsmen who can quickly move onto the attack; a number three of wonderful flair, to whom a maiden over is an insult; a middle order which can provide both 'concrete' and aggression; a late middle order of 'big guns'; and a tail whose achievements with the bat make a mockery of that description.

Add to these qualities of batting and bowling close catching and outfielding second to none in the country, unparalleled running between the wickets and wicket-keeping of the very highest quality, and you have a championship side that can rival even the Yorkshire sides of the 1930s, with every component delicately balanced.

These winning components give to a side a corporate personality, and a sense of efficiency, but they are incomplete in themselves. Over and above them must be the individual character of each player which will mould into the character of the side and yet transcend it.

The great Yorkshire sides of the thirties mentioned above have left a lasting impression of dour, ruthless efficiency, of success achieved in unsmiling fashion. This was the corporate image, but consider the individuals — the sartorial, unruffled elegance of Herbert Sutcliffe; the humorous pragmatism of Maurice Leyland; the scholastic artistry of Hedley Verity; the spectacled fire of Bill Bowes; and, later than these, the grace and charm of Len Hutton.

The Essex side of 1979 has left an image of bubbling happiness, but it left, too, memories of generous and warm human beings as vulnerable as the rest of us.

One remembers shaking hands with Alf Gooch, Graham's father, during the Benson and Hedges final at Lord's and saying nothing, because there was nothing left to say. And there was Graham himself with that forlorn moustache which makes him look like one who is still bewildered that he has had greatness thrust upon him. In the Prudential World Cup match at Lord's, against Australia, he fielded fine leg at the Nursery End and wore a mournful look as if surprised to find himself in such august company, and then he went out to bat with England at 5 for 2, and within minutes we wondered why we had ever doubted that England would win.

Mike Denness had arrived at Essex with over 20,000 runs and 28 Test matches behind him, but scarred by some of the vicissitudes of cricket. He had treated the two imposters of triumph and disaster just the same, and now the twinkling eyes and the quiet calm of the elder statesman brought a wisdom to Essex cricket, but this state of *éminence grise* attained through some measure of pain was linked to a youthful zest to prove that he still had more than most to offer on the field of play itself.

Like Denness, Stuart Turner had known heartache and disappointment, but there is no greater fighter. He bristles with endeavour, determined to snatch every moment from the game which is his life. He lives every ball with an agony of concentration, and proves those wrong who once said he wasn't good enough with every ball he bowls and every shot he hits. It is unlikely now that he will ever win an England cap, but to those who follow the three-day game, the heart of cricket, he is one of the very best of English county cricketers.

Of a different mould is David Acfield. He has accomplished much in many walks of life. Not as extrovert as many of his colleagues on the field, he spins on with thoughtful wit, a perfect foil to the zaniness of Ray East.

'A fellow of infinite jest', and endeavour, arms flailing in all directions like a broken-down windmill, Ray East does not play *to* the gallery, he is *of* the gallery. A great iconoclast, he has even done a music hall turn with David Constant's white hat. Ray

East has provided a constant reminder to those who need it that cricket is fun.

The personalities of Ken McEwan and Norbert Phillip are revealed more in their style of performance than in any theatricalities. By nature they are quiet and shy men though no less sociable than their companions. They are students of the game who have brought a necessary dimension to Essex cricket. McEwan's batting is like Virginia Woolf's writing, liquid and transparent, delicate to the touch. Phillip's cricket is the harnessed fire of the introvert. It is one of the criminal follies of the modern world that Ken McEwan will probably never play a Test innings at Lord's. What a joy that would have been!

Neil Smith is also a shy man. His observation and his comment are perceptive, but he offers them with humility. He has grown from boyhood to manhood at Essex, but he has never quite lost the sense of boyish wonder that he is at Essex at all. He lights up when he dismisses a batsman, but almost immediately subsides into quietude as if apologising for having made a fuss. His business-like efficiency has never caught the eye of selectors or critics, but that is their loss. Here is one of the best of wicketkeepers, and a man with singleness of purpose, dedicated to his art. A batsman of tremendous power, with an expert short-arm punch, he leaves the field after a good knock with an embarrassed smile as if surprised that all those people have been watching.

Another who has undergone a process of maturation over the past few years is Keith Pont. Schoolboy star is not always the best preparation for becoming a county cricketer, but he has navigated the inevitable problems to establish himself as a popular young man of immense talent. The gods of cricket have had their sport with him in the past, but one feels now that his Ithaca cannot be too far away.

Brian Hardie navigated his problems to become an indispensable batsman and a short-leg fielder in a class of his own, and through his trials he never lost his sense of humour, or his singularity with regard to his after-match drink, lager.

In 1980, John Lever takes his benefit, and one is willing to wager that the public's response will be very generous. Wholehearted, fresh, intelligent, happy in his and the team's achivement, John Lever has stamped his personality indelibly upon Essex cricket. It is sufficient to say of him that when his fellow cricketers voted as to who should win the Reg Hayter Cup for The Cricketers' Cricketer of the Year Award in 1979, John Lever polled more votes than all the other contenders put together. There is no finer judgement of a man than the views of those who work with him every day.

It became customary in 1979 for the press to describe Keith Fletcher as the 'gnome'. Their use of the title was obscure. Did they intend to suggest that his slight stoop in the field gave him pixie-like qualities or did they mean specifically the dictionary definition, 'super-physical being, of diminutive size, the guardian of precious metals hidden in the earth', or did they simply refer to the utterance of wise sayings? Probably they meant all three. There are still those outside the County who minimise the man's worth; but a man is what he is. His splendid Test record has passed almost unnoticed. He left the Test scene just before the arrival of the lucrative rewards that have been earned by some lesser players to-day. You will never see him pictured in only jock strap and pads in an Australian cricket magazine to advertise cricket gear, as you will see Tony Greig. Fletcher will remain quiet and effectual, and in the last analysis, many will look at his record and say, 'I didn't realise he was that good.' But his colleagues realise it, and they respect the man and his judgement.

If one had to single out one man to thank for the achievements of 1979 that man would be Keith Fletcher. Above all, he insisted that what was accomplished was accomplished professionally, and with fun.

'And the great thing was, we all felt part of it.'

Appendix

Full Statistics
of all matches played by Essex County
Cricket Club in the summer of 1979

*The author is indebted to the work of
Clem Driver and Leslie Newnham in the
compilation of these statistics*

K.W.R. Fletcher captained the side in
every game, and Neil Smith kept wicket
in every game. For the opponents,
the captain is marked †
and the wicket-keeper *

The Schweppes County Championship
and other first-class matches

There was no play possible in the match between Surrey and Essex at The Oval, 26, 28 and 29 May

Schweppes County Champtionship 1979

	p	w	l	d	Bonus Pts bt	bl	pts
Essex	22	13	4	5	56	69	281
Worcestershire	22	7	4	11	58	62	204
Surrey	22	6	3	13	50	70	192
Sussex	22	6	4	12	47	65	184
Kent	22	6	3	13	49	60	181
Leicestershire	22	4	5	13	60	68	176
Yorkshire	22	5	3	14	52	63	175
Somerset	22	5	1	16	56	55	171
Nottinghamshire	22	6	4	12	43	54	169
Gloucestershire	22	5	4	13	53	54	167
Northamptonshire	22	3	6	13	59	58	153
Hampshire	22	3	9	10	39	66	141
Lancashire	22	4	4	14	37	55	140
Middlesex	22	3	3	16	44	60	140
Warwickshire	22	3	7	12	46	51	133
Derbyshire	22	1	6	15	46	60	118
Glamorgan	22	0	10	12	35	58	93

v KENT AT CHELMSFORD
2, 3 and 4 May

Essex	First innings		Second innings	
M.H. Denness	b Hills	37	c Knott, b Jarvis	0
G.A. Gooch	b Jarvis	13	lbw, b Underwood	11
K.S. McEwan	c Johnson, b Shepherd	20	c Knott, b Jarvis	0
K.W.R. Fletcher	c Tavare, b Hills	41	c Hills, b Johnson	4
B.R. Hardie	c Tavare, b Hills	15	c Shepherd, b Johnson	4
K.R. Pont	c Woolmer, b Shepherd	33	c Cowdrey, b Underwood	0
S. Turner	c Hills, b Shepherd	102	c Ealham, b Johnson	6
N. Phillip	not out	39	not out	3
N. Smith	not out	0	c Shepherd, b Johnson	0
J.K. Lever			c Knott, b Johnson	12
D.L. Acfield				
	lb 3, nb 2	5	lb 1, nb 2	3
	for 7 wkts, dec	305	for 9 wkts	43

	O	M	R	W	O	M	R	W
Jarvis	16	2	77	1	5	4	4	2
Shepherd	28	4	81	3	6	2	11	—
Hills	23	6	59	3				
Underwood	20	7	45	—	8	4	13	2
Johnson	3	—	38	—	6.1	3	12	5

fall of wickets
1– 17, 2– 55, 3– 86, 4– 128, 5– 129, 6– 204, 7– 304
1– 0, 2– 0, 3– 15, 4– 15, 5– 19, 6– 19, 7– 26, 8– 26, 9– 43

Kent	First innings	
R.A. Woolmer	c Hardie, b Phillip	29
C.J.C. Rowe	not out	108
C.J. Tavare	c Smith, b Pont	34
C.S. Cowdrey	c Turner, b Phillip	19
† A.G.E. Ealham	c Lever, b Phillip	15
J.N. Shepherd	c Smith, b Pont	19
* A.P.E. Knott	lbw, b Acfield	1
R.W. Hills	b Acfield	0
D.L. Underwood	not out	8
G.W. Johnson	c Smith, b Pont	0
K.B.S. Jarvis		
	lb 10, w 1, nb 6	17
	for 8 wkts	250

	O	M	R	W
Lever	20	6	36	–
Phillip	24	12	37	3
Turner	32	11	79	–
Acfield	9	2	28	2
Pont	20	6	44	3
Gooch	5	2	9	–

fall of wickets
1– 63, 2– 122, 3– 160, 4– 176, 5– 220, 6– 220, 7– 224, 8– 230

Umpires – A. Jepson and D. Dennis

Match drawn
Essex 6 pts, Kent 5 pts

Essex won the toss

v. MIDDLESEX AT LORD'S
9, 10 and 11 May

Middlesex	First innings	
†J.M. Brearley	c Gooch, b Lever	73
M.J. Smith	st Smith, b East	33
C.T. Radley	lbw, b East	5
G.D. Barlow	lbw, b Lever	45
M.W. Gatting	c Hardie, b Phillip	17
*I.J. Gould	run out	0
P.H. Edmonds	not out	40
J.E. Emburey	not out	33
M.W.W. Selvey		
W.W. Daniel		
A.A. Jones		
	b 8, lb 8, w 1, nb 2	19
	for 6 wkts, dec	265

	O	M	R	W
Lever	22	4	51	2
Phillip	17	5	42	1
Turner	17	6	25	–
East	29	7	99	2
Acfield	14.1	4	29	–

fall of wickets
1– 76, 2– 84, 3– 141, 4– 176, 5– 176, 6– 220

Essex	*First innings*	
M.H. Denness	lbw, b Selvey	19
G.A. Gooch	lbw, b Daniel	8
K.S. McEwan	b Selvey	66
K.W.R. Fletcher	c Brearley, b Emburey	32
B.R. Hardie	not out	40
R.E. East	c Edmonds, b Jones	30
S. Turner	c Gatting, b Daniel	2
N. Phillip	b Emburey	13
N. Smith	not out	0
J.K. Lever		
D.L. Acfield		
	b 5, lb 1, nb 8	14
	for 7 wkts	224

	O	M	R	W
Selvey	23	8	61	2
Daniel	18	—	61	2
Emburey	18	4	32	2
Jones	14	1	37	1
Edmonds	7	—	19	—

fall of wickets

1– 26, 2– 38, 3– 88, 4– 159, 5– 186, 6– 195, 7– 212

Umpires – C.T. Spencer and P.B. Wight

Match abandoned as a draw, no play on the last day
Middlesex 6 pts, Essex 4 pts

Middlesex won the toss

v DERBYSHIRE AT CHESTERFIELD
16, 17 and 18 May

Essex	*First innings*	
G.A. Gooch	b Barnett	109
M.H. Denness	c Kirsten, b Russell	10
K.S. McEwan	c Tunnicliffe, b Walters	21
K.W.R. Fletcher	not out	140
B.R. Hardie	run out	35
K.R. Pont	not out	6
S. Turner, N. Phillip,		
N. Smith, J.K. Lever and D.L. Acfield did not bat		
	lb 9, w 1, nb 4	14
	for 4 wkts	335

	O	M	R	W
Hendrick	24	5	52	—
Tunnicliffe	19	6	56	—
Russell	23	6	74	1
Walters	13	1	48	1
Miller	12	2	52	—
Barnett	7	2	23	1
Kirsten	2	—	16	—

fall of wickets
1– 21, 2– 58, 3– 206, 4– 316

Derbyshire	*First innings*		*Second innings*	
A.J. Borrington	c Smith, b Phillip	19	c Hardie, b Lever	10
J.G. Wright	b Lever	0	c Hardie, b Lever	13
P.E. Russell	c Fletcher, b Phillip	4	c Smith, b Lever	0
†D.S. Steele	c Hardie, b Turner	11	lbw, b Lever	0
P.N. Kirsten	c McEwan, b Phillip	6	c Fletcher, b Turner	0
G. Miller	c Smith, b Turner	2	lbw, b Turner	0
K. Barnett	c Fletcher, b Turner	1	c Turner, b Lever	19
J. Walters	lbw, b Phillip	1	c Denness, b Turner	0
C.J. Tunnicliffe	c Turner, b Phillip	2	c Gooch, b Phillip	39
'R.W. Taylor	c Gooch, b Lever	5	c Pont, b Lever	6
M. Hendrick	not out	4	not out	0
	lb 3, w 3, nb 2	8	b 4, lb 4, nb 6	14
		63		101

	O	M	R	W	O	M	R	W
Lever	7.3	—	20	2	24	10	52	6
Phillip	12	1	23	5	9.5	5	9	1
Turner	9	3	12	3	11	6	20	3
Acfield					4	1	6	—

fall of wickets
1– 1, 2– 23, 3– 24, 4– 43, 5– 46, 6– 47, 7– 48, 8– 48, 9– 52
1– 32, 2– 32, 3– 35, 4– 35, 5– 37, 6– 37, 7– 44, 8– 89, 9– 97

Umpires – A.E. Rhodes and T.W. Spencer

Essex won by an innings and 171 runs
Essex 20 pts, Derbyshire 1 pt

Essex won the toss

v GLAMORGAN AT ILFORD
1 June (there was no play possible on 30 and 31 May)

Glamorgan	*First innings*	
A. Jones	b Lever	36
J.A. Hopkins	c Turner, b Lever	9
R.C. Ontong	c and b Hardie	86
A.L. Jones	c Phillip, b Fletcher	17
P.D. Swart	retired hurt	16
M.J. Llewellyn	c Lever, b Hardie	5
G. Richards	c Phillip, b Fletcher	5
*E.W. Jones	not out	0
A.E. Cordle	c and b Fletcher	4
B.J. Lloyd	not out	0
†R.N.S. Hobbs		
	w 1, nb 5	6
	for 7 wkts, dec	184

	O	M	R	W
Lever	16	4	29	2
Phillip	7	2	16	—
Turner	7	5	3	—
Acfield	17	8	15	—
East	16	6	32	—
Fletcher	7	—	44	3
Hardie	5	—	39	2

fall of wickets
1— 19, 2— 66, 3— 127, 4— 169, 5— 180, 6— 180, 7— 184

Essex	*First innings*	
M.H. Denness	c Ontong, b Cordle	14
G.A. Gooch	not out	93
K.S. McEwan	not out	67

K.W.R. Fletcher, B.R. Hardie, S. Turner,
R.E. East, N. Phillip, N. Smith,
J.K. Lever and D.L. Acfield did not bat

	b 5, lb 6	11
	for 1 wkt	185

	O	M	R	W
Cordle	11	—	62	1
Ontong	8.3	1	62	—
Lloyd	2	—	14	—
Richards	6	—	36	—

fall of wicket
1— 44

Umpires — A. Jepson and C. Cook

Essex won by 9 wickets
Essex 12 pts in match reduced to one innings

Glamorgan won the toss

v LANCASHIRE AT ILFORD
2 and 4 June

Essex	*First innings*	
M.H. Denness	b Lee	30
G.A. Gooch	c Lyon, b Hogg	23
K.S. McEwan	b Reidy	88
K.W.R. Fletcher	b Lee	8
B.R. Hardie	not out	100
S. Turner	b Hogg	25
N. Phillip	lbw, b Wood	14
N. Smith	not out	30

R.E. East, J.K. Lever and D.L. Acfield did not bat

	b 9, lb 8, nb 4	21
	for 6 wkts, dec	339

	O	M	R	W
Hogg	17	4	63	2
Lee	18.1	4	54	2
Wood	15	2	46	1
Arrowsmith	7	—	45	—
Reidy	18	2	61	1
Simmons	17	2	49	—

fall of wickets
1— 50, 2— 65, 3— 115, 4— 191, 5— 245, 6— 283

Lancashire	*First innings*		*Second innings*	
B. Wood	b Lever	7	c Smith, b Lever	34
A. Kennedy	c Gooch, b Lever	14	lbw, b Phillip	11
D. Lloyd	c Smith, b Lever	2	c Turner, b Gooch	14
†F.C. Hayes	b Lever	0	c Smith, b Lever	10
J. Abrahams	c Smith, b Lever	0	c McEwan, b Turner	6
B.W. Reidy	b Lever	16	b Acfield	28
J. Simmons	c Gooch, b Turner	4	c Fletcher, b Turner	0
*J. Lyon	not out	19	b Acfield	9
R. Arrowsmith	b Phillip	5	not out	0
W. Hogg	b Turner	11	c Smith, b Acfield	0
P.G. Lee	b Lever	0	b Acfield	0
	lb 2, nb 4	6	b 2, lb 2, w 4, nb 3	11
		84		123

	O	M	R	W	O	M	R	W
Lever	14	2	27	7	14	6	22	2
Phillip	12	3	32	1	7	3	11	1
Turner	7	4	6	2	14	8	19	2
East	3	—	13	—	21	8	28	—
Gooch					6	—	21	1
Acfield					6	2	11	4

fall of wickets
1— 15, 2— 22, 3— 22, 4— 25, 5— 31, 6— 44, 7— 46, 8— 54, 9— 83
1— 22, 2— 51, 3— 75, 4— 82, 5— 95, 6— 101, 7— 120, 8— 123, 9— 123

Umpires — A. Jepson and C. Cook

Essex won by an innings and 132 runs
Essex 20 pts, Lancashire 2 pts

Essex won the toss

v LEICESTERSHIRE AT CHELMSFORD
9, 11 and 12 June

Essex	First innings		Second innings	
M.H. Denness	c Clift, b Shuttleworth	122	lbw, b Taylor	3
M.S.A. McEvoy	b Higgs	21	c Davison, b Higgs	0
K.S. McEwan	b Shuttleworth	4	b Taylor	39
K.W.R. Fletcher	lbw, b Shuttleworth	1	c Higgs, b Taylor	0
B.R. Hardie	c Shuttleworth, b Higgs	30	c Briers, b Taylor	40
S. Turner	c Tolchard, b Higgs	0	b Shuttleworth	46
N. Phillip	c Steele, b Higgs	0	c Shuttleworth, b Taylor	27
N. Smith	not out	90	c Tolchard, b Taylor	6
R.E. East	run out	5	run out	0
J.K. Lever	c Shuttleworth, b Higgs	4	not out	7
D.L. Acfield	not out	5	b Clift	6
	b 4, lb 10, nb 7	21	lb 6, nb 1	7
	for 9 wkts	303		181

	O	M	R	W	O	M	R	W
Taylor	21	6	47	—	17	3	61	6
Higgs	25	6	72	5	10	3	22	1
Shuttleworth	29	6	102	3	8	—	33	1
Clift	17	5	42	—	11.4	4	13	1
Steele	8	1	19	—	6	2	15	—
Cook					5	2	14	—
Balderstone					4	1	16	—

fall of wickets
1— 63, 2— 72, 3— 77, 4— 156, 5— 157, 6— 157, 7— 249, 8— 256, 9— 288
1— 2, 2— 8, 3— 10, 4— 57, 5— 116, 6— 154, 7— 167, 8— 167, 9— 170

Leicestershire	First innings		Second innings	
N.E. Briers	c Turner, b Phillip	10	c Smith, b Phillip	1
J.F. Steele	c Turner, b Lever	20	c McEvoy, b Lever	11
B. Dudleston	c Smith, b Turner	48	lbw, b Lever	18
B.F. Davison	c Hardie, b Lever	72	b Phillip	67
J.C. Balderstone	b Lever	28	b Lever	4
*R.W. Tolchard	c Hardie, b Lever	1	c Turner, b Lever	4
P.B. Clift	c Smith, b East	25	b Lever	0
N.G.B. Cook	c Turner, b Lever	0	b Lever	1
K. Shuttleworth	not out	17	b Phillip	23
†K. Higgs	c Turner, b Lever	0	not out	5
L.B. Taylor	c McEvoy, b East	0	lbw, b Taylor	0
	lb 7, nb 4	11	lb 9, w 1, nb 9	19
		232		153

	O	M	R	W	O	M	R	W
Lever	23	4	76	6	16.1	5	41	7
Phillip	12	2	27	1	17	6	55	3
Turner	10	5	30	1	7	2	15	—
East	21.4	7	51	2	7	1	23	—
Acfield	16	6	37	—				

fall of wickets
1— 25, 2— 50, 3— 100, 4— 178, 5— 184, 6— 187, 7— 194, 8— 230, 9— 231
1— 4, 2— 27, 3— 33, 4— 47, 5— 64, 6— 64, 7— 66, 8— 133, 9— 148

Umpires — D. J. Dennis and P.S.G. Stevens

Essex won by 99 runs
Essex 20 pts, Leicestershire 6 pts

Essex won the toss

v WARWICKSHIRE AT EDGBASTON
13, 14 and 15 June

Warwickshire	First innings		Second innings	
D.L. Amiss	c McEvoy, b Lever	56	b Lever	7
K.D. Smith	lbw, b Lever	7	b East	40
†J. Whitehouse	b Lever	1	c McEwan, b Lever	25
T.A. Lloyd	c McEvoy, b Turner	15	b Lever	36
P.R. Oliver	c Hardie, b Lever	6	c McEwan, b Lever	0
R.N. Abberley	lbw, b Lever	15	b East	1
*C.W. Maynard	c Turner, b Lever	18	c McEwan, b Lever	0
C.C. Clifford	b Lever	0	c Hardie, b East	2
S.P. Perryman	c Denness, b Lever	6	b Phillip	11
D.C. Hopkins	b Turner	34	c Hardie, b East	4
R. Le Q. Savage	not out	14	not out	0
	b 1, lb 5, nb 7	13	b 1, lb 7	8
		185		134

	O	M	R	W		O	M	R	W
Lever	30	10	49	8		19	7	38	5
Phillip	22	7	56	–		14	2	36	1
Turner	24.3	8	43	2		3	1	2	–
East	13	3	24	–		29.3	12	34	4
Acfield						13	7	16	–

fall of wickets
1– 15, 2– 18, 3– 78, 4– 87, 5– 94, 6– 113, 7– 119, 8– 125, 9– 140
1– 10, 2– 67, 3– 98, 4– 98, 5– 103, 6– 108, 7– 115, 8– 119, 9– 134

Essex	*First innings*	
M.H. Denness	b Hopkins	34
M.S.A. McEvoy	lbw, b Perryman	0
R.E. East	c Maynard, b Clifford	49
K.S. McEwan	not out	208
K.W.R. Fletcher	c Maynard, b Hopkins	64
B.R. Hardie	c Maynard, b Hopkins	10
S. Turner	c Abberley, b Savage	4
N. Phillip	b Hopkins	10
N. Smith	not out	0

J.K. Lever and D.L Acfield did not bat

	lb 10, w 2, nb 3	15
	for 7 wkts, dec	394

	O	M	R	W
Perryman	12	2	30	1
Hopkins	26.4	1	106	4
Clifford	13	1	72	1
Savage	28	4	103	1
Oliver	16	3	56	–
Lloyd	2	–	12	–

fall of wickets
1– 1, 2– 86, 3– 94, 4– 313, 5– 337, 6– 362, 7– 394

Umpires – J.V.C. Griffiths and R. Julian

Essex won by an innings and 75 runs
Essex 20 pts, Warwickshire 4 pts

Warwickshire won the toss

v SOMERSET AT BATH
16, 18 and 19 June

Somerset	First innings		Second innings	
†B.C. Rose	c Smith, b Phillip	28	c Fletcher, b Phillip	1
P.W. Denning	c McEvoy, b Turner	21	b Lever	10
P.M. Roebuck	lbw, b Turner	50	c Phillip, b Lever	12
M.J. Kitchen	c East, b Phillip	34	c Smith, b Lever	8
V.J. Marks	not out	70	b East	93
P.A. Slocombe	c Smith, b Lever	20	c McEwan, b Turner	22
D. Breakwell	lbw, b Acfield	14	not out	54
*D.J.S. Taylor	lbw, b Acfield	5	not out	12
C.H. Dredge	b Phillip	18	c McEwan, b East	55
K.F. Jennings	lbw, b Acfield	0	not out	12
H.R. Moseley	not out	0		
	b 6, lb 8, nb 3	17	b 4, lb 4, w 1, nb 8	17
	for 9 wkts	277	for 7 wkts, dec	284

	O	M	R	W	O	M	R	W
Lever	20	1	40	1	20	4	61	3
Phillip	18	2	70	3	22	7	54	1
East	4	1	10	—	18.2	2	37	2
Turner	30	5	80	2	17	6	46	1
Acfield	28	9	60	3	18	2	69	—

fall of wickets
1– 39, 2– 71, 3– 88, 4– 144, 5– 189, 6– 230, 7– 244, 8– 244, 9– 277
1– 1, 2– 34, 3– 46, 4– 55, 5– 63, 6– 203, 7– 242

Essex	First innings		Second innings	
M.H. Denness	c Roebuck, b Breakwell	39	c Taylor, b Moseley	0
M.S.A. McEvoy	st Taylor, b Jennings	5	c Roebuck, b Dredge	2
R.E. East	c Marks, b Moseley	70	not out	1
K.S. McEwan	b Breakwell	71	lbw, b Dredge	18
K.W.R. Fletcher	c Taylor, b Dredge	14	lbw, b Moseley	34
B.R. Hardie	b Moseley	54	c Taylor, b Moseley	14
S. Turner	c Taylor, b Moseley	14	c Rose, b Moseley	3
N. Phillip	not out	17	not out	8
N. Smith	c Taylor, b Moseley	1	c Taylor, b Moseley	0
J.K. Lever	not out	1		
D.L. Acfield				
	b 4, lb 12	16	b 4, lb 2, w 1	7
	for 8 wkts	302	for 7 wkts	87

	O	M	R	W	O	M	R	W
Moseley	28	10	52	4	14.4	6	18	5
Dredge	21	3	60	1	17	6	35	2
Jennings	17	5	56	1				
Breakwell	24	5	83	2	9	4	10	–
Marks	10	–	35	–	5	–	17	–

fall of wickets
1– 14, 2– 96, 3– 159, 4– 197, 5– 211, 6– 279, 7– 288, 8– 292
1– 1, 2– 11, 3– 28, 4– 70, 5– 74, 6– 81, 7– 82

Umpires – J.V.C. Griffiths and R. Julian

Match drawn
Essex 8 pts, Somerset 6 pts

Somerset won the toss

v DERBYSHIRE AT CHELMSFORD
20, 21 and 22 June

Derbyshire	*First innings*		*Second innings*	
A. Hill	lbw, b Lever	10	b Lever	19
I.S. Anderson	b Phillip	2	lbw, b Lever	0
†D.S. Steele	lbw, b Phillip	4	c Hardie, b Phillip	5
P.N. Kirsten	b Lever	11	c Denness, b Turner	3
A.J. Borrington	c Smith, b Phillip	12	lbw, b East	34
K.J. Barnett	c Smith, b Lever	0	c Smith, b Lever	21
F.W. Swarbrook	c Smith, b Turner	52	b Phillip	5
J. Walters	c Pont, b Lever	54	c East, b Lever	9
C.J. Tunnicliffe	b Phillip	57	not out	18
R.C. Wincer	lbw, b Lever	3	b Phillip	3
*A. McLellan	not out	8	c Smith, b Phillip	0
	b 5, lb 24, w 3, nb 9	45	b 4, lb 5, w 2, nb 9	20
		258		137

	O	M	R	W	O	M	R	W
Lever	30	5	72	5	18	4	45	4
Phillip	26.4	11	59	4	10	–	28	4
Turner	27	6	51	1	15	7	27	1
Pont	11	2	29	–				
East	3	1	2	–	15	7	17	1

fall of wickets
1– 4, 2– 14, 3– 28, 4– 29, 5– 43, 6– 53, 7– 138, 8– 208, 9– 215
1– 1, 2– 18, 3– 28, 4– 36, 5– 95, 6– 95, 7– 109, 8– 126, 9– 131

Essex	*First innings*	
M.H. Denness	c Steele, b Walters	35
A.W. Lilley	c Barnett, b Tunnicliffe	0
R.E. East	c McLellan, b Wincer	19
K.S. McEwan	c Steele, b Kirsten	185
K.W.R. Fletcher	c Steele, b Wincer	15
B.R. Hardie	c McLellan, b Kirsten	7
K.R. Pont	c McLellan, b Kirsten	77
S. Turner	b Walters	43
N. Phillip	c Barnett, b Tunnicliffe	6
N. Smith	not out	16
J.K. Lever did not bat		
	b 3, lb 15, nb 14	32
	for 9 wkts, dec	435

	O	M	R	W
Wincer	20	3	84	2
Tunnicliffe	19	6	74	2
Walters	33	6	120	2
Steele	6	–	39	–
Swarbrook	3	–	28	–
Kirsten	18.2	3	58	3

fall of wickets
1– 0, 2– 39, 3– 170, 4– 232, 5– 278, 6– 280, 7– 293, 8– 375, 9– 435

Umpires – H.D. Bird and B.J. Meyer

Essex won by an innings and 40 runs
Essex 20 pts, Derbyshire 7 pts

Derbyshire won the toss

v KENT AT TUNBRIDGE WELLS
23 June (no play possible on 25 and 26 June)

Kent	*First innings*	
R.A. Woolmer	c Smith, b Turner	23
C.J.C. Rowe	c Hardie, b Lever	3
C.J. Tavare	not out	150
C.S. Cowdrey	c McEwan, b Turner	51
†A.G. Ealham	b East	14
J.N. Shepherd	c Hardie, b East	4
G.W. Johnson	b Lever	25
*A.P.E. Knott	lbw, b Lever	1
D.L. Underwood	c McEwan, b Turner	23
G.R. Dilley		
K.B.S. Jarvis		
	lb 10, nb 12	22
	for 8 wkts, dec	316

	O	M	R	W
Lever	26	5	73	3
Phillip	15	1	63	–
Turner	25.5	6	70	3
East	32	10	88	2

fall of wickets
1– 13, 2– 38, 3– 151, 4– 172, 5– 196, 6– 256, 7– 264, 8– 316

Essex	*First innings*	
M.H. Denness	not out	10
A.W. Lilley	lbw, b Underwood	6
R.E. East	not out	2

K.S. McEwan, K.W.R. Fletcher, B.R. Hardie,
K.R. Pont, S. Turner, N. Phillip, N. Smith,
and J.K. Lever did not bat

		nb 2	2
		for 1 wkt.	20

	O	M	R	W
Dilley	5	2	9	–
Jarvis	4	2	7	–
Underwood	1	–	2	1

fall of wicket
1– 18

Umpires – W.E. Alley and D.G.L. Evans

Match drawn
Kent 4 pts, Essex 3 pts

Kent won the toss

v SUSSEX AT SOUTHEND
7, 9 and 10 July

Essex	*First innings*			*Second innings*	
M.H. Denness	st Long, b Waller	136		not out	4
G.A. Gooch	c Barclay, b Phillipson	86		not out	5
K.S. McEwan	c Long, b Arnold	29			
K.W.R. Fletcher	not out	52			
B.R. Hardie	lbw, b Phillipson	1			
K.R. Pont	b Waller	17			

N. Phillip, S. Turner, N. Smith,
R.E. East and J.K. Lever did not bat

	lb 6, nb 11	17		b 2, w 1	3
	for 5 wkts, dec	338		for no wkt	12

	O	M	R	W		O	M	R	W
Imran Khan	17	4	61	–	1	1	0	–
Arnold	19	3	50	1				
Phillipson	21	4	55	2				
Spencer	14	2	51	–				
Waller	22.3	3	79	2				
Barclay	6	1	25	–	1	–	9	–

fall of wickets
1– 170, 2– 230, 3– 292, 4– 295, 5– 338

Sussex	*First innings*		*Second innings*	
K.C. Wessels	c Smith, b Lever	21	c Turner, b Lever	33
J.R.T. Barclay	c Fletcher, b Turner	40	c Hardie, b Lever	3
G.D. Mendis	lbw, b Lever	19	c East, b Phillip	0
P.W.G. Parker	c McEwan, b Phillip	13	c Gooch, b Lever	41
Imran Khan	c Gooch, b Phillip	1	c Smith, b Lever	2
P.J. Graves	c Smith, b Phillip	0	c McEwan, b Pont	16
C.P. Phillipson	c Smith, b Turner	6	lbw, b Turner	42
G.G. Arnold	b Phillip	14	c Smith, b Phillip	21
†*A. Long	not out	5	c Smith, b Phillip	2
J. Spencer	b Lever	4	c Fletcher, b Phillip	9
C.E. Waller	c Gooch, b Turner	6	not out	8
	lb 9, w 1, nb 4	14	b 1, lb 8, w 3, nb 15	27
		143		204

	O	M	R	W	O	M	R	W
Lever	20	5	46	3	24	7	67	4
Phillip	17	8	42	4	19	5	55	4
Turner	15	5	17	3	17	6	29	1
East	1	–	5	–	6	3	10	–
Pont	7	1	19	–	6	1	16	1

fall of wickets
1– 28, 2– 52, 3– 71, 4– 78, 5– 82, 6– 100, 7– 126, 8– 130, 9– 136
1– 15, 2– 18, 3– 71, 4– 81, 5– 82, 6– 124, 7– 155, 8– 160, 9– 180

Umpires – R. Herman and K.E. Palmer

Essex won by 10 wickets
Essex 20 pts, Sussex 2 pts

Essex won the toss

v NOTTINGHAMSHIRE AT SOUTHEND
11, 12 and 13 July

Essex	First innings		Second innings	
M.H. Denness	c Curzon, b Hacker	65	lbw, b Bore	7
A.W. Lilley	c Harris, b Hacker	35	c Hassan, b Rice	5
K.S. McEwan	b Bore	13	c Hadlee, b Rice	14
K.W.R. Fletcher	b Hemmings	28	c Mackintosh, b Bore	43
B.R. Hardie	c Smedley, b Bore	11	c Mackintosh, b Hadlee	8
K.R Pont	lbw, b Hadlee	18	b Bore	10
N. Phillip	c Smedley, b Hemmings	18	c Hassan, b Bore	40
S. Turner	c Curzon, b Hadlee	18	not out	68
N. Smith	c Hacker, b Hadlee	20	c Hadlee, b Hemmings	2
R.E. East	c Hassan, b Bore	4	c Rice, b Bore	0
D.L. Acfield	not out	0	hit wkt, b Hadlee	10
	b 5, lb 5	10	b 5, lb 10, w 5, nb 2	22
		240		229

	O	M	R	W	O	M	R	W
Hadlee	15	3	49	4	24	4	51	2
Rice	5	–	15	–	16	3	42	2
Mackintosh	10	3	23	–				
Hacker	7	–	37	1				
Bore	29.5	15	55	3	35	11	79	5
Hemmings	17	6	51	2	21	7	35	1

fall of wickets
1– 66, 2– 106, 3– 122, 4– 159, 5– 159, 6– 187, 7– 208, 8– 225, 9– 238
1– 13, 2– 27, 3– 31, 4– 55, 5– 80, 6– 113, 7– 179, 8– 186, 9– 187

Nottinghamshire	First innings		Second innings	
M.J. Harris	b Phillip	9	lbw, b East	18
B. Hassan	c Pont, b East	32	c Hardie, b Acfield	49
†M.J. Smedley	lbw, b Phillip	34	b Acfield	16
C.E.B. Rice	c Lilley, b East	86	c and b East	2
H.T. Tunnicliffe	run out	56	c Fletcher, b East	11
K.F. Mackintosh	lbw, b Phillip	8	c Acfield, b East	8
E.E. Hemmings	c Turner, b Acfield	5	lbw, b Acfield	0
R.J. Hadlee	c McEwan, b East	31	c Hardie, b East	0
*C.C. Curzon	not out	18	not out	10
M.K. Bore	c Smith, b East	0	lbw, b Acfield	3
P.J. Hacker	lbw, b Acfield	3	c Hardie, b Acfield	0
	lb 14, nb 4	18	b 2, lb 3, w 1	6
		300		123

	O	M	R	W	O	M	R	W
Phillip	22	6	54	3	5	–	20	–
Turner	17	2	54	–	6	2	13	–
East	40	9	93	4	24	7	56	5
Acfield	32.5	7	81	2	23.2	12	28	5

fall of wickets
1– 24, 2– 65, 3– 109, 4– 197, 5– 237, 6– 245, 7– 247, 8– 295, 9– 295
1– 40, 2– 87, 3– 88, 4– 92, 5– 109, 6– 110, 7– 110, 8– 110, 9– 115

Umpires – R. Herman and K.E. Palmer

Essex won by 46 runs
Essex 17 pts, Nottinghamshire 7 pts

Essex won the toss

v HAMPSHIRE AT BOURNEMOUTH
25, 26 and 27 July

Hampshire	*First innings*		*Second innings*	
C.G. Greenidge	c Smith, b Lever	26	lbw, b East	67
J.M. Rice	b Turner	9	c Hardie, b Acfield	49
D.R. Turner	c McEvoy, b Turner	5	c Smith, b East	16
T.E. Jesty	c McEvoy, b Turner	16	b Acfield	6
D.J. Rock	b Lever	16	b East	8
N.G. Cowley	lbw, b Lever	3	c Smith, b Acfield	12
M.N.S. Taylor	c Smith, b Lever	5	c East, b Acfield	11
†*G.R. Stephenson	c Smith, b Lever	19	c Hardie, b Acfield	7
M.D. Marshall	c Gooch, b Lever	5	c McEvoy, b East	16
M.J. Bailey	not out	4	c Smith, b Phillip	19
K. Stevenson	c McEwan, b Phillip	0	not out	0
	b 4, lb 16	20	b 1, lb 6, nb 1	8
		128		219

	O	M	R	W	O	M	R	W
Lever	23	7	40	7	14	4	38	–
Phillip	16.3	3	44	1	13.3	1	52	1
Turner	14	7	24	2	6	1	12	–
Acfield					30	10	61	5
East					23	8	48	4

fall of wickets
1– 40, 2– 44, 3– 48, 4– 73, 5– 77, 6– 87, 7– 88, 8– 104, 9– 127
1– 117, 2– 121, 3– 133, 4– 135, 5– 147, 6– 158, 7– 182, 8– 186, 9– 215

Essex	First innings	
G.A. Gooch	c Stephenson, b Marshall	70
M.S.A. McEvoy	c Bailey, b Taylor	9
K.S. McEwan	c Stephenson, b Marshall	29
K.W.R. Fletcher	b Marshall	20
B.R. Hardie	not out	146
N. Phillip	b Marshall	0
S. Turner	lbw, b Stevenson	15
N. Smith	c Stephenson, b Stevenson	14
R.E. East	c Rock, b Jesty	48
J.K. Lever	c Marshall, b Cowley	2
D.L. Acfield	c Jesty, b Stevenson	10
	b 7, lb 4, w 1, nb 5	17
		380

	O	M	R	W
Marshall	30	8	93	4
Stevenson	29.5	7	83	3
Jesty	15	3	72	1
Taylor	13	4	39	1
Rice	4	–	15	–
Cowley	11	2	45	1
Bailey	3	–	16	–

fall of wickets
1– 42, 2– 103, 3– 118, 4– 157, 5– 161, 6– 186, 7– 208, 8– 322, 9– 380

Umpires – D.J. Constant and R. Julian

Essex won by an innings and 33 runs
Essex 20 pts, Hampshire 4 pts

Hampshire won the toss

v GLOUCESTERSHIRE AT CASTLE PARK, COLCHESTER
28, 30 and 31 July (no play on last day; extra half-hour on 30 July)

Gloucestershire	First innings		Second innings	
A.W. Stovold	c Smith, b East	47	c Acfield, b Lever	52
Sadiq Mohammad	c Fletcher, b Phillip	5	lbw, b East	15
Zaheer Abbas	c Gooch, b Lever	0	c Smith, b Turner	29
A.J. Hignell	c Denness, b Lever	0	c Hardie, b Acfield	30
†M.J. Proctor	c Fletcher, b Lever	8	c Fletcher, b Acfield	0
P. Bainbridge	lbw, b Lever	0	c Hardie, b Acfield	4
M.D. Partridge	c Denness, b Phillip	8	c Fletcher, b Acfield	0
D.A. Graveney	c Gooch, b Acfield	7	b Acfield	23
*A.J. Brassington	b Acfield	3	c Smith, b Acfield	4
B.M. Brain	st Smith, b East	3	c Gooch, b Phillip	24
J.H. Childs	not out	0	not out	2
	b 5, lb 1, nb 5	11	b 8, lb 9, nb 5	22
		92		205

	O	M	R	W	O	M	R	W
Lever	10	2	37	4	11	3	30	1
Phillip	12	–	28	2	5.5	1	16	1
Turner	5	1	11	–	6	1	19	1
East	5	4	1	2	38	18	62	1
Acfield	4	2	4	2	40	15	56	6

fall of wickets
1– 19, 2– 20, 3– 20, 4– 43, 5– 47, 6– 74, 7– 80, 8– 89, 9– 92
1– 30, 2– 71, 3– 138, 4– 140, 5– 144, 6– 144, 7– 145, 8– 159, 9– 193

Essex	First innings		Second innings	
M.H. Denness	c Hignell, b Brain	1	c Sadiq, b Graveney	44
G.A. Gooch	lbw, b Brain	6	c Hignell, b Partridge	7
K.S. McEwan	c Stovold, b Childs	10	c Brassington, b Graveney	1
K.W.R. Fletcher	c Hignell, b Brain	0	c sub, b Childs	33
B.R. Hardie	c Hignell, b Brain	14	c and b Graveney	11
N. Smith	c Partridge, b Brain	0		
N. Phillip	c Brassington, b Graveney	62	c Hignell, b Graveney	0
S. Turner	c Sadiq, b Childs	35	not out	8
R.E. East	b Childs	15	not out	10
J.K. Lever	st Brassington, b Childs	9		
D.L. Acfield	not out	5		
	b 4, lb 6, nb 3	13	b 8, lb 5, nb 2	15
		170	for 6 wkts	129

	O	M	R	W	O	M	R	W
Brain	9	–	35	5	2	–	7	–
Procter	6	2	10	–	7	1	16	–
Childs	18	4	82	4	14	5	28	1
Graveney	9.1	–	32	1	17.5	3	58	4
Partridge					2	–	5	1

fall of wickets
1– 4, 2– 7, 3– 7, 4– 37, 5– 37, 6– 37, 7– 106, 8– 132, 9– 148
1– 23, 2– 28, 3– 89, 4– 108, 5– 119, 6– 119

Umpires – J.G. Langridge and D.O. Oslear

Essex won by 4 wickets
Essex 17 pts, Gloucestershire 4 pts

Gloucestershire won the toss

v MIDDLESEX AT CASTLE PARK, COLCHESTER
1, 2 and 3 August

Essex	First innings		Second innings	
M.H. Denness	lbw, b Selvey	0	lbw, b Selvey	3
M.S.A. McEvoy	c Gould, b Selvey	7	c Gould, b Daniel	0
K.S. McEwan	b Daniel	24	c Butcher, b Daniel	8
K.W.R. Fletcher	lbw, b Selvey	0	c Radley, b Titmus	57
B.R. Hardie	b Daniel	41	c Gould, b Selvey	30
K.R. Pont	c Featherstone, b Daniel	0	c Radley, b Featherstone	59
N. Phillip	c Gould, b Daniel	7	lbw, b Featherstone	28
S. Turner	c Butcher, b Selvey	12	b Daniel	11
N. Smith	c Radley, b Daniel	0	c Gatting, b Featherstone	10
R.E. East	not out	6	b Featherstone	8
D.L. Acfield	c Gould, b Daniel	1	not out	0
	lb 2, nb 6	8	lb 4, nb 7	11
		106		225

	O	M	R	W	O	M	R	W
Daniel	12.2	6	38	6	18	2	75	3
Selvey	13	7	20	4	10	5	45	2
Jones	7	1	25	–	10	–	34	–
Titmus	6	3	15	–	9	1	32	1
Featherstone					5.4	–	28	4

fall of wickets
1– 5, 2– 8, 3– 9, 4– 58, 5– 58, 6– 78, 7– 92, 8– 92, 9– 104
1– 3, 2– 3, 3– 17, 4– 61, 5– 130, 6– 191, 7– 194, 8– 215, 9– 216

Middlesex	First innings		Second innings	
M.J. Smith	c Fletcher, b East	33	not out	21
M.W. Gatting	lbw, b East	39	not out	12
†C.T. Radley	c Hardie, b Fletcher	55		
G.D. Barlow	c Fletcher, b East	10		
N.G. Featherstone	lbw, b Phillip	3		
R.O. Butcher	c McEvoy, b East	29		
*I.J. Gould	c Acfield, b Fletcher	34		
M.W. Selvey	c Phillip, b Fletcher	45		
F.J. Titmus	c McEvoy, b Fletcher	25		
W.W. Daniel	b Fletcher	2		
A.A. Jones	not out	1		
	b 5, lb 3, w 3, nb 12	23	lb 2, w 1	3
		299	for no wkt	36

	O	M	R	W	O	M	R	W
Phillip	18	2	69	1	2	–	14	–
Turner	6	1	18	–	3.1	–	14	–
East	44	11	106	4				
Acfield	22	6	42	–				
Fletcher	15.3	3	41	5				
Pont					2	1	5	–

fall of wickets
1– 76, 2– 85, 3– 113, 4– 116, 5– 163, 6– 205, 7– 238, 8– 290, 9– 294

Umpires – J.G. Langridge and D.O. Oslear

Middlesex won by 9 wickets
Middlesex 19 pts, Essex 3 pts

Essex won the toss

v WORCESTERSHIRE AT WORCESTER
4, 6 and 7 August

Worcestershire	First innings	
G.M. Turner	c Pont, b Turner	9
J.A. Ormrod	st Smith, b East	134
P.A. Neale	c Denness, b Acfield	25
E.J.O. Hemsley	b Acfield	27
Younis Ahmed	b Phillip	37
D.N. Patel	c Acfield, b East	14
*D.J. Humphries	c East, b Phillip	37
J.D. Inchmore	not out	21
V.A. Holder	lbw, b Phillip	16
†N. Gifford	c Fletcher, b East	6
J. Cumbes		
	b 8, lb 4, nb 15	27
	for 9 wkts	353

	O	M	R	W
Phillip	19	4	55	3
Turner	11	2	38	1
Acfield	37	10	105	2
East	33	7	128	3

fall of wickets
1– 19, 2– 72, 3– 132, 4– 199, 5– 248, 6– 302, 7– 316, 8– 338, 9– 353

Essex	First innings		Second innings	
M.H. Denness	c Humphries, b Cumbes	39	lbw, c Cumbes	11
B.R. Hardie	lbw, b Holder	33	c Patel, b Inchmore	35
K.S. McEwan	b Holder	7	c Holder, b Inchmore	9
K.W.R. Fletcher	c Ormrod, b Gifford	18	lbw, b Inchmore	4
K.R. Pont	c Patel, b Gifford	18	c Humphries, b Inchmore	4
M.S.A. McEvoy	lbw, b Cumbes	6	c Humphries, b Holder	28
N. Phillip	c Humphries, b Cumbes	10	c Neale, b Gifford	1
S. Turner	lbw, b Gifford	13	c Humphries, b Holder	4
R.E. East	b Cumbes	9	c Hemsley, b Inchmore	19
N. Smith	c sub, b Cumbes	4	c and b Inchmore	10
D.L. Acfield	not out	1	not out	0
	b 6, lb 12, w 1, nb 8	27	b 4, lb 7, w 1, nb 9	21
		185		146

	O	M	R	W	O	M	R	W
Holder	21	3	39	2	20	6	53	2
Inchmore	6	–	12	–	14.4	3	35	6
Patel	4	–	9	–				
Gifford	34	14	67	3	13	5	27	1
Cumbes	18	5	31	5	10	4	10	1

fall of wickets
1– 75, 2– 88, 3– 113, 4– 121, 5– 138, 6– 151, 7– 166, 8– 177, 9– 182
1– 46, 2– 54, 3– 64, 4– 69, 5– 72, 6– 73, 7– 87, 8– 133, 9– 138

Umpires – P.B. Wight and B.J. Meyer

Worcestershire won by an innings and 22 runs
Worcestershire 20 pts, Essex 5 pts

Worcestershire won the toss

v NORTHAMPTONSHIRE AT NORTHAMPTON
18, 20 and 21 August

Northamptonshire	First innings		Second innings	
W. Larkins	lbw, b Lever	0	lbw, b Lever	17
G. Cook	lbw, b Turner	32	b Turner	38
R.G. Williams	b Phillip	1	lbw, b Lever	1
A.J. Lamb	c Hardie, b Phillip	2	lbw, b Phillip	66
P. Willey	lbw, b Turner	131	lbw, b Turner	2
T.J. Yardley	b Turner	1	c Denness, b Phillip	24
*G. Sharp	lbw, b Lever	9	lbw, b Turner	2
†P.J. Watts	c Fletcher, b Turner	12	not out	25
Sarfraz Nawaz	b Turner	5	lbw, b Turner	0
T.M. Lamb	not out	3	b Turner	2
B.J. Griffiths	c Smith, b Phillip	3	lbw, b Lever	2
	b 4, lb 12, w 2, nb 7	25	b 2, lb 13, w 1, nb 8	24
		224		203

	O	M	R	W	O	M	R	W
Lever	22	4	77	2	22.3	4	71	3
Phillip	17.4	6	35	3	15	2	52	2
Turner	17	2	70	5	25	2	56	5
Acfield	13	4	17	—				
East					2	2	0	—

fall of wickets
1— 1, 2— 7, 3— 9, 4— 71, 5— 83, 6— 149, 7— 205, 8— 216, 9— 219
1— 35, 2— 41, 3— 104, 4— 106, 5— 161, 6— 166, 7— 174, 8— 174, 9— 195

Essex	*First innings*		*Second innings*	
M.H. Denness	c Yardley, b Sarfraz	31	b Williams	51
B.R. Hardie	lbw, b Sarfraz	11	not out	103
K.S. McEwan	lbw, b Sarfraz	70	lbw, b Willey	11
K.W.R. Fletcher	not out	52	c Yardley, b Larkins	39
K.R. Pont	c Yardley, b Griffiths	6	not out	8
S. Turner	lbw, b Griffiths	6		
N. Phillip	b Sarfraz	2		
N. Smith	b Sarfraz	0		
R.E. East	c Yardley, b Sarfraz	3		
J.K. Lever	run out	1		
D.L. Acfield	c Sharp, b Griffiths	0		
	b 1, lb 6, w 2, nb 8	17	b 1, lb 16	17
		199	for 3 wkts	229

	O	M	R	W	O	M	R	W
Sarfraz	27	7	60	6	7	2	23	—
Griffiths	23.4	6	65	3	21	5	55	—
T.M. Lamb	19	6	35	—	12	4	23	—
Willey	10	4	22	—	28	7	42	1
Williams					15	5	29	1
Larkins					7	3	15	1
Watts					5	1	22	—
Yardley					0.3	—	3	—

fall of wickets
1— 22, 2— 118, 3— 121, 4— 143, 5— 157, 6— 165, 7— 169, 8— 183, 9— 187
1— 113, 2— 132, 3— 210

Umpires — P.B. Wight and K.E. Palmer

Essex won by 7 wickets
Essex 17 pts, Northamptonshire 6 pts

Essex won the toss and asked Northamptonshire to bat

v SURREY AT CHELMSFORD
25, 27 and 28 August

Essex	First innings		Second innings	
G.A. Gooch	c Richards, b Jackman	5	b Wilson	9
M.H. Denness	c Richards, b Jackman	61	c Howarth, b Knight	29
K.S. McEwan	b Knight	22	c Richards, b Wilson	11
K.W.R. Fletcher	c Roope, b Jackman	4	c Knight, b Wilson	13
B.R. Hardie	b Pocock	76	c Howarth, b Jackman	4
K.R. Pont	c Richards, b Jackman	7	c Howarth, b Roope	11
S. Turner	c Butcher, b Wilson	11	not out :	6
N. Phillip	c Lynch, b Pocock	66	c Richards, b Roope	0
N. Smith	b Pocock	0	c Butcher, b Jackman	1
R.E. East	not out	25	c Roope, b Jackman	3
J.K. Lever	not out	11	c Richards, b Jackman	3
	b 1, lb 9, nb 2	12	lb 9, nb 2	11
	for 9 wkts	300		101

	O	M	R	W		O	M	R	W
Jackman	30	8	88	4		17.1	4	37	4
Wilson	24	6	67	1		14	3	38	3
Knight	18	5	56	1		6	1	10	1
Roope	5	—	17	—		3	2	5	2
Pocock	23	4	60	3					

fall of wickets
1– 13, 2– 42, 3– 47, 4– 130, 5– 146, 6– 164, 7– 242, 8– 246, 9– 267
1– 22, 2– 34, 3– 40, 4– 64, 5– 69, 6– 87, 7– 87, 8– 87, 9– 93

Surrey	First innings		Second innings	
A.R. Butcher	lbw, b Turner	11	c Gooch, b Lever	24
G.S. Clinton	lbw, b Phillip	6	c Smith, b Lever	11
G.P. Howarth	c Fletcher, b Turner	103	c Gooch, b Lever	15
†R.D.V. Knight	c Smith, b Turner	42	c Smith, b Turner	1
G.R.J. Roope	lbw, b Lever	61	lbw, b Turner	0
M.A. Lynch	lbw, b Lever	4	c McEwan, b Phillip	0
R.D. Jackman	lbw, b Turner	0	b Phillip	9
Intikhab Alam	c Pont, b Phillip	14	not out	16
*C.J. Richards	c Pont, b Phillip	2	b Phillip	3
P.I. Pocock	b Lever	20	c Fletcher, b Lever	5
P.H.L. Wilson	not out	1	b Phillip	6
	b 5, lb 11, w 1, nb 6	23	b 2, lb 6, nb 1	9
		287		99

	O	M	R	W		O	M	R	W
Lever	28	5	83	3		20	4	54	4
Phillip	20	5	52	3		12.5	3	19	4
Turner	24	7	61	4		7	2	17	2
Pont	11	2	41	–					
East	14	7	27	–					

fall of wickets
1– 16, 2– 46, 3– 159, 4– 180, 5– 187, 6– 192, 7– 228, 8– 236, 9– 282
1– 6, 2– 35, 3– 40, 4– 40, 5– 44, 6– 61, 7– 63, 8– 68, 9– 78

Umpires – W.E. Alley and R. Aspinall

Essex won by 15 runs
Essex 20 pts, Surrey 7 pts

Essex won the toss

v NORTHAMPTONSHIRE AT CHELMSFORD
29, 30 and 31 August

Northamptonshire	*First innings*		*Second innings*	
G. Cook	c and b Phillip	10	lbw, b Sainsbury	0
W. Larkins	c Hardie, b Acfield	91	lbw, b Turner	23
R.G. Williams	c McEwan, b East	22	c Smith, b Turner	51
A.J. Lamb	run out	69	c McEvoy, b Turner	2
T.J Yardley	lbw, b Phillip	13	c McEwan, b Phillip	36
R.M. Carter	c Sainsbury, b Acfield	10	c Smith, b Turner	3
*G. Sharp	c Smith, b Turner	30	c and b Acfield	7
†P.J. Watts	not out	36	b Turner	1
A. Hodgson	not out	7	c McEwan, b Acfield	1
T.M. Lamb			not out	0
B.J. Griffiths			b Phillip	0
	b 8, lb 8, w 1, nb 9	26	b 1, lb 5, w 1, nb 6	13
	for 7 wkts	314		137

	O	M	R	W		O	M	R	W
Phillip	13	1	60	2		10.3	4	34	2
Sainsbury	12	–	41	–		11	2	38	1
Turner	23	2	60	1		17	1	39	5
Acfield	30	3	66	2		7	2	13	2
East	22	3	61	1					

fall of wickets
1– 18, 2– 91, 3– 157, 4– 195, 5– 225, 6– 235, 7– 292
1– 5, 2– 39, 3– 41, 4– 115, 5– 121, 6– 130, 7– 131, 8– 132, 9– 137

Essex	First innings		Second innings	
M.H. Denness	lbw, b Hodgson	4	b T. Lamb	30
B.R. Hardie	c A. Lamb, b Griffiths	93	b Griffiths	17
K.S. McEwan	c Sharp, b Griffiths	30	c A. Lamb, b T. Lamb	18
K.W.R. Fletcher	c Sharp, b Griffiths	2	not out	50
M.S.A. McEvoy	lbw, b Hodgson	24	lbw, b T. Lamb	6
N. Phillip	c Cook, b Hodgson	4	c Sharp, b T. Lamb	11
S. Turner	lbw, b Griffiths	12	not out	15
N. Smith	c Larkins, b T. Lamb	63		
R.E. East	c Cook, b Griffiths	47		
D.L. Acfield	not out	12		
G. Sainsbury				
	b 4, lb 6, w 1, nb 1	12	b 2, lb 4, w 1	7
	for 9 wkts, dec	303	for 5 wkts	154

	O	M	R	W	O	M	R	W
Griffiths	26.3	5	76	5	17	3	39	1
Hodgson	18	–	96	3	6	1	22	–
T.M. Lamb	14	2	56	1	17	4	60	4
Larkins	9	3	20	–				
Williams	13	4	43	–				
Carter					5	2	10	–
Cook					1.2	–	16	–

fall of wickets
1– 7, 2– 84, 3– 86, 4– 142, 5– 150, 6– 170, 7– 189, 8– 280
1– 29, 2– 50, 3– 70, 4– 94, 5– 118

Umpires – W.E. Alley and R. Aspinall

Essex won by 5 wickets
Essex 19 pts, Northamptonshire 8 pts

Northamptonshire won the toss

v LEICESTERSHIRE AT LEICESTER
1, 3 and 4 September

Leicestershire	First innings		Second innings	
B. Dudleston	lbw, b Turner	62	b Lever	20
J.F. Steele	lbw, b Acfield	56	not out	107
J.C. Balderstone	b Acfield	55	not out	66
B.F. Davison	lbw, b East	27		
N.E. Briers	c Phillip, b East	15		
P.B. Clift	c Turner, b East	23		
†*R.W. Tolchard	not out	39		
J. Birkenshaw	run out	1		
P. Booth	not out	12		
N.G.B. Cook and J.P. Agnew did not bat				
	b 2, lb 13, nb 5	20	b 10, lb 20, nb 3	33
	for 7 wkts	310	for 1 wkt, dec	226

	O	M	R	W		O	M	R	W
Lever	12	4	42	–		20.4	1	54	1
Phillip	7	1	21	–		6	–	23	–
Turner	13	5	22	1		17	4	37	–
Acfield	38	5	125	2		20	8	38	–
East	30	6	80	3		23	7	41	–

fall of wickets
1– 96, 2– 149, 3– 208, 4– 222, 5– 235, 6– 272, 7– 274
1– 40

Essex	*First innings*		*Second innings*	
M.H. Denness	c Tolchard, b Booth	16	c Tolchard, b Cook	28
B.R. Hardie	c Tolchard, b Birkenshaw	45	not out	59
K.S. McEwan	c Steele, b Birkenshaw	21	c Birkenshaw, b Cook	2
K.W.R. Fletcher	b Cook	21	b Cook	1
K.R. Pont	c and b Birkenshaw	0	c Davison, b Cook	18
N. Phillip	b Cook	13	c Birkenshaw, b Cook	0
S. Turner	run out	1	c Cook, b Balderstone	39
N. Smith	b Clift	11	st Tolchard, b Cook	9
R.E. East	c Tolchard, b Cook	9	c sub, b Birkenshaw	3
J.K. Lever	b Clift	3	c Birkenshaw, b Balderstone	4
D.L. Acfield	not out	5	st Tolchard, b Birkenshaw	0
	b 9, lb 6, w 1, nb 6	22	lb 8, nb 1	9
		167		172

	O	M	R	W		O	M	R	W
Agnew	10	5	23	–		5	1	14	–
Booth	9	3	24	1					
Clift	16	4	37	2		7	3	12	–
Cook	25.5	10	41	3		26	12	57	6
Birkenshaw	9	3	20	3		25.3	8	67	2
Balderstone						4	–	13	2

fall of wickets
1– 37, 2– 98, 3– 99, 4– 99, 5– 132, 6– 134, 7– 150, 8– 150, 9– 153
1– 54, 2– 56, 3– 60, 4– 80, 5– 82, 6– 147, 7– 151, 8– 168, 9– 172

Umpires – W.L. Budd and D.O. Oslear

Leicestershire won by 197 runs
Leicestershire 20 pts, Essex 4 pts

Leicestershire won the toss

v YORKSHIRE AT SCARBOROUGH
5, 6 and 7 September

Essex	First innings		Second innings	
M.H. Denness	c Bairstow, b Carrick	35	st Athey, b Carrick	25
G.A. Gooch	c Bairstow, b Sidebottom	69	c Cope, b Sidebottom	21
B.R. Hardie	b Sidebottom	8	b Old	16
K.S. McEwan	c Lumb, b Stevenson	124	c sub, b Carrick	14
K.W.R. Fletcher	c Lumb, b Stevenson	50	c Athey, b Stevenson	40
S. Turner	c Hampshire, b Old	2	c Old, b Sidebottom	4
N. Phillip	b Old	17	c Athey, b Carrick	1
N. Smith	b Stevenson	10	lbw, b Sidebottom	0
R.E. East	c Hartley, b Stevenson	5	c sub, b Carrick	0
J.K. Lever	not out	1	c Stevenson, b Carrick	14
D.L. Acfield			not out	0
	b 2, lb 5, nb 11	18	b 7, lb 10, nb 2	19
	for 9 wkts, dec	339		154

	O	M	R	W	O	M	R	W
Old	24.3	7	51	2	20	4	43	1
Stevenson	26	10	61	4	10	4	13	1
Sidebottom	20	4	75	2	15	8	18	3
Carrick	16	4	70	1	32.3	15	61	5
Cope	11	1	59	—				
Love	1	—	5	—				

fall ot wickets
1– 111, 2– 113, 3– 122, 4– 298, 5– 303, 6– 303, 7– 320, 8– 337, 9– 339
1– 50, 2– 64, 3– 78, 4– 87, 5– 109, 6– 110, 7– 111, 8– 124, 9– 154

Yorkshire	First innings		Second innings	
R.G. Lumb	c Denness, b East	110	c Hardie, b Lever	14
C.W.J. Athey	c Hardie, b Lever	13	lbw, b Turner	19
J.D. Love	c Smith, b Lever	28	lbw, b Turner	22
P. Carrick	c and b East	59	b Turner	32
S.N. Hartley	c and b Lever	39	lbw, b Acfield	0
†J.H. Hampshire	not out	39	lbw, b Acfield	21
*D.L. Bairstow	c and b East	9	hit wkt, b Phillip	15
A. Sidebottom	not out	1	c Smith, b Turner	0
G.B. Stevenson			not out	23
C.M. Old			c McEwan, b Turner	0
G.A. Cope			not out	5
	b 15, lb 10, nb 6	31	b 8, lb 4, nb 4	16
	for 6 wkts, dec	329	for 9 wkts	167

	O	M	R	W	O	M	R	W
Lever	20	5	74	3	9	3	15	1
Phillip	13	2	40	–	12.5	1	42	1
Turner	18	5	37	–	14	4	35	5
Gooch	13	2	45	–				
Acfield	16	4	78	–	15	3	36	2
East	17	3	54	3	7	2	23	–

fall of wickets
1– 22, 2– 77, 3– 195, 4– 262, 5– 289, 6– 328
1– 29, 2– 41, 3– 85, 4– 91, 5– 95, 6– 95, 7– 103, 8– 132, 9– 134

Umpires – J. Van Geloven and R. Julian

Yorkshire won by 1 wicket
Yorkshire 20 pts, Essex 6 pts

Essex won the toss
C.W.J. Athey kept wicket for Yorkshire in the second innings

Other First-Class Matches

v CAMBRIDGE UNIVERSITY AT FENNER'S, CAMBRIDGE
21, 23 and 24 April

Cambridge University	*First innings*		*Second innings*	
A.M. Mubarak	b Turner	25	lbw, b Lever	2
J.P.C. Mills	c Gooch, b Pont	11	lbw, b Pont	27
D.C. Holliday	c Gooch, b Pont	3	c Hardie, b Turner	1
A.R. Dewes	lbw, b Turner	3	c and b Gooch	38
M.D.W. Edwards	c Gooch, b Pont	18	not out	7
D.R. Pringle	lbw, b Gooch	2	not out	11
†I.A. Greig	c Hardie, b Acfield	46		
N.C. Crawford	c Gooch, b Turner	4		
N.F.M. Popplewell	b Acfield	35		
*P.R. Cottrell	lbw, b Lever	26		
D. Surridge	not out	10		
	b 2, lb 12	14	b 1, lb 3	4
		197	for 4 wkts	90

	O	M	R	W	O	M	R	W
Lever	18.4	2	67	1	8	4	12	1
Pont	16	3	34	3	7	1	15	1
Turner	17	6	26	3	8	4	11	1
Gooch	4	1	10	1	7	2	14	1
East	10	3	20	–	10	3	17	–
Acfield	17	5	26	2	7	1	17	–

fall of wickets
1– 29, 2– 38, 3– 40, 4– 46, 5– 49, 6– 72, 7– 79, 8– 154, 9– 197
1– 2, 2– 3, 3– 64, 4– 76

Essex	*First innings*	
G.A. Gooch	c Cottrell, b Surridge	33
A.W. Lilley	run out	30
K.S. McEwan	c Cottrell, b Popplewell	49
K.W.R. Fletcher	b Crawford	56
B.R. Hardie	c Holliday, b Pringle	59
K.R. Pont	b Pringle	10
S. Turner	c Edwards, b Surridge	36
R.E. East	c Pringle, b Surridge	11
N. Smith	not out	9

J.K. Lever and D.L. Acfield did not bat

	b 6, lb 9	15
	for 8 wkts, dec	308

	O	M	R	W
Surridge	26.1	4	73	3
Greig	15	3	36	–
Pringle	29	8	79	2
Popplewell	18	3	69	1
Holliday	3	2	6	–
Crawford	7	2	30	1

fall of wickets
1– 64, 2– 70, 3– 156, 4– 184, 5– 211, 6– 286, 7– 291, 8– 308

Umpires – W.L. Budd and C.T. Spencer

Match drawn

Cambridge University won the toss

v INDIA AT CHELMSFORD
11, 12 and 13 August

Essex	*First innings*		*Second innings*	
M.H. Denness	c Reddy, b Amarnath	1	c Gavaskar, b Chandra	58
G.A. Gooch	c Gavaskar, b Dev	0	c Bedi, b Venkat	46
K.S. McEwan	c Gavaskar, b Bedi	16	b Bedi	68
K.W.R. Fletcher	b Chandra	64	c Reddy, b Venkat	6
B.R. Hardie	c Gavaskar, b Chandra	0	c Chauhan, b Bedi	0
K.R. Pont	c Reddy, b Vankat	4	not out	40
N. Phillip	c Gavaskar, b Bedi	1	not out	7
S. Turner	b Venkat	0		
N. Smith	c Sharma, b Chandra	46	c Bedi, b Chauhan	65
J.K. Lever	not out	1		
D.L. Acfield	b Chandra	0		
	lb 7, w 3, nb 3	13	lb 2, w 1, nb 2	5
		146	for 6 wkts, dec	295

	O	M	R	W	O	M	R	W
Kapil Dev	15	3	46	1	9	3	27	–
Amarnath	7	4	10	1	7	1	17	–
Bedi	22	12	19	2	25	5	78	2
Chandrasekhar	9.2	1	30	4	19	–	72	1
Venkataraghavan	14	5	28	2	24	9	65	2
Chauhan					4	1	21	1
Gavaskar					2	–	10	–

fall of wickets
1– 2, 2– 2, 3– 31, 4– 39, 5– 53, 6– 54, 7– 55, 8– 145, 9– 146
1– 72, 2– 84, 3– 142, 4– 224, 5– 224, 5– 248

India	First innings		Second innings	
S.M. Gavaskar	c Smith, b Phillip	1	c Smith, b Lever	8
C.P.S. Chauhan	lbw, b Phillip	10	c Gooch, b Fletcher	28
D.B. Vengsarkar	lbw, b Phillip	5		
Y. Sharma	c Hardie, b Lever	111	not out	39
M. Amarnath	b Pont	55	not out	42
Kapil Dev	c McEwan, b Phillip	4		
*B. Reddy	c Smith, b Lever	16		
†S. Venkataraghavan	run out	0		
B.S. Bedi	not out	2		

A.D. Gaekwad and B.S. Chandrasekhar did not bat

	b 4, lb 4, nb 3	11	b 6, lb 6, nb 3	15
	for 8 wkts, dec	215	for 2 wkts	132

	O	M	R	W	O	M	R	W
Lever	23.4	6	67	2	9	–	25	1
Phillip	18	3	50	4	7	1	11	–
Turner	13	3	36	–	1	–	1	–
Pont	9	1	28	1	7	–	20	–
Acfield	7	3	7	–	5	2	7	–
Gooch	6	1	16	–	2	1	4	–
Fletcher					12	2	49	1

fall of wickets
1– 9, 2– 14, 3– 19, 4– 115, 5– 153, 6– 201, 7– 201, 8– 215
1– 21, 2– 68

Umpires – K.E. Palmer and D. Shackleton

Match drawn

Essex won the toss

*Essex in the Schweppes County Championship
and other First-Class Matches 1979*

Schweppes County Championship Matches: played 21; won 13; drawn 4; lost 4.
abandoned 1.
Position in Championship: first.
Other first-class matches: played 2; drawn 2.

BATTING AVERAGES IN SCHWEPPES COUNTY CHAMPIONSHIP MATCHES

	Matches	Inns	NO	Runs	HS	Av.	100s	50s	0s
B.R. Hardie	21	31	5	1111	146*	42.73	3	4	—
K.S. McEwan	21	32	2	1254	208*	41.80	3	5	1
G.A. Gooch	10	15	2	535	109	41.15	1	4	—
K.W.R. Fletcher	21	31	4	880	140*	32.59	1	6	3
M.H. Denness	20	33	2	973	136	31.38	2	3	3
S. Turner	21	28	4	525	102	21.87	1	1	1
R.E. East	19	25	5	390	70	19.50	—	1	3
K.R. Pont	11	17	2	292	77	19.46	—	2	3
N. Phillip	21	28	4	417	66	17.37	—	2	5
N. Smith	21	26	6	297	90*	14.85	—	2	7
A.W. Lilley	3	4	0	46	35	11.50	—	—	1
D.L. Acfield	17	15	9	55	12*	9.16	—	—	2
M.S.A. McEvoy	7	12	0	108	28	9.00	—	—	3
J.K. Lever	17	13	4	72	14	8.00	—	—	—
G.E. Sainsbury	1	—	—	—	—	—	—	—	—

Scoring Rate
Essex scored 7431 runs from 14373 balls at a rate of 51.70 per 100 balls or 3.10 per over.

Striking Rate
Opponents took 261 wickets at a rate of 55.07 balls per wicket.

BOWLING AVERAGES IN SCHWEPPES COUNTY CHAMPIONSHIP MATCHES

	M	I	O	Mdns	R	W	Av	5wI	10wM	Best
K.W.R. Fletcher	21	2	22.3	3	85	8	10.62	1	—	5—41
J.K. Lever	17	30	575.5	138	1460	99	14.74	8	2	8—49
B.R. Hardie	21	1	5	0	39	2	19.50	—	—	2—39
S. Turner	21	37	537.3	151	1211	57	21.24	4	1	5—35
N. Phillip	21	37	523.1	124	1445	66	21.89	1	—	5—23
D.L. Acfield	17	23	453.2	132	991	39	25.41	3	—	6—56
R.E. East	19	29	541.3	162	1253	43	29.13	1	—	5—56
K.R. Pont	11	6	57	13	154	4	38.50	—	—	3—44
G.A. Gooch	10	3	24	4	75	1	75.00	—	—	1—21
G.E. Sainsbury	1	2	23	2	79	1	79.00	—	—	1—38

Scoring Rate
Opponents scored 7444 runs from 16577 balls at a rate of 44.91 per 100 balls or 2.69 per over.

Striking Rate
Essex took 324 wickets at a rate of 51.16 balls per wicket.

Over Rate
Over rate per hour: first half of season 18.68; second half of season 19.29
total 19.02.

BATTING AVERAGES IN ALL FIRST-CLASS MATCHES

Cap		Matches	Inns	NO	Runs	HS	Av	100s	50s	Os
1974	K.S. McEwan	23	35	2	1387	208*	42.03	3	6	1
1974	B.R. Hardie	23	34	5	1170	146*	40.34	3	5	2
1975	G.A. Gooch	12	18	2	614	109	38.37	1	4	1
1963	K.W.R. Fletcher	23	34	4	1006	140*	33.53	1	8	3
1977	M.H. Denness	21	35	2	1032	136	31.27	2	4	3
1970	S. Turner	23	30	4	561	102	21.57	1	1	2
1976	K.R. Pont	13	20	3	346	77	20.35	—	2	3
1967	R.E. East	20	26	5	401	70	19.09	—	1	3
1975	N. Smith	23	29	7	417	90*	18.95	—	3	7
1978	N. Phillip	22	30	5	425	66	17.00	—	2	5
—	A.W. Lilley	4	5	0	76	35	15.20	—	—	1
—	M.S.A. McEvoy	7	12	0	108	28	9.00	—	—	3
1970	J.K. Lever	19	14	5	73	14	8.11	—	—	—
1970	D.L. Acfield	19	16	9	55	12*	7.85	—	—	3
—	G.E. Sainsbury	1	—	—	—	—	—	—	—	—

Runs		7671
Byes		108
Leg byes		241
Wides		22
No balls		138

	Matches	Inns	NO	Runs	HS	Av	100s	50s	Os
TOTALS	23	338	53	8180	208*	28.70	11	36	37

Mode of Dismissal

	B	C & B	Caught	Ct sub	Ct WK	St	Lbw	Hit Wkt	Run Out	Total
McEwan	10	—	12	1	7	—	3	—	—	33
Hardie	6	1	13	—	5	—	3	—	1	29
Gooch	3	—	5	—	5	—	3	—	—	16
Fletcher	7	—	13	1	5	—	4	—	—	30
Denness	5	—	10	—	9	2	7	—	—	33
Turner	5	—	12	—	4	—	4	—	1	26
Pont	3	1	8	—	4	—	1	—	—	17
East	3	—	11	2	3	—	—	—	2	21
Smith	4	1	10	1	4	1	1	—	—	22
Phillip	6	—	11	—	6	—	2	—	—	25
Lilley	—	—	3	—	—	—	1	—	1	5
McEvoy	1	—	3	—	3	1	4	—	—	12
Lever	1	—	4	—	2	1	—	—	1	9
Acfield	2	—	1	—	2	1	—	1	—	7
Totals	56	3	116	5	59	6	33	1	6	285

Scoring Rate
Runs scored from 15906 balls at a rate of 51.43 per 100 balls or 3.09 per over.

Striking Rate
Opponents took wickets at a rate of 55.81 balls per wicket.

BOWLING AVERAGES IN ALL FIRST-CLASS MATCHES

	Type	M	I	O	Mdns	R	W	Av	5wI	10wM	Best
K.W.R. Fletcher	LB	23	3	34.3	5	134	9	14.88	1	–	5–41
J.K. Lever	LFM	19	34	635.1	150	1631	104	15.68	8	2	8–49
B.R. Hardie	RM	23	1	5	0	39	2	19.50	–	–	2–39
S. Turner	RFM	23	41	576.3	164	1285	61	21.06	4	1	5–35
N. Phillip	RFM	22	39	548.1	128	1506	70	21.51	1	–	5–23
D.L. Acfield	OB	19	27	489.2	143	1048	41	25.56	3	–	6–56
K.R. Pont	RM	13	10	96	18	251	9	27.88	–	–	3–34
R.E. East	SLA	20	31	561.3	168	1290	43	30.00	1	–	5–56
G.A. Gooch	RM	12	7	43	9	119	3	39.66	–	–	1–10
G.E. Sainsbury	LFM	1	2	23	2	79	1	79.00	–	–	1–38

Runs					7382	343	21.52	
Byes					139			
Leg byes					310			
Wides					32			
No balls					215			
Run outs						5		

	M	I	O	Mdns	R	W	Av	5wI	10wM	Best
TOTALS	23	41	3012.1	787	8078	348	23.21	18	3	8–49

Mode of Dismissal

	B	C & B	Ct	Ct sub	Ct WK	St	Lbw	Hit Wkt	Total	Run Out
Fletcher	1	1	7	–	–	–	–	–	9	
Lever	22	1	41	–	18	–	22	–	104	
Hardie	–	1	1	–	–	–	–	–	2	
Turner	10	–	23	–	12	–	16	–	61	
Phillip	17	1	28	–	11	–	12	1	70	
Acfield	11	1	16	–	3	–	10	–	41	
Pont	1	–	4	–	3	–	1	–	9	
East	5	3	21	–	4	3	7	–	43	
Gooch	–	1	1	–	–	–	1	–	3	
Sainsbury	–	–	–	–	–	–	1	–	1	
Totals	67	9	142	–	51	3	70	1	343	5

Scoring Rate
Opponents scored their runs from 18073 balls at a rate of 44.70 per 100 balls or 2.68 per over.

Striking Rate
Wickets were taken at a rate of 51.93 balls per wicket.

CATCHES AND STUMPINGS

N. Smith   51 catches   3 stumpings

B.R. Hardie	30 catches		R.E. East	8 catches
G.A. Gooch	20		N. Phillip	6
K.W.R. Fletcher	19		K.R. Pont	6
K.S. McEwan	19		D.L. Acfield	5
S. Turner	14		J.K. Lever	3
M.S.A. McEvoy	11		A.W. Lilley	1
M.H. Denness	8		G.E. Sainsbury	1

HIGHEST TOTAL

For: 435—9 dec v Derbyshire at Chelmsford.
Against: 353—9 in 100 overs v Worcestershire
          at Worcester.

LOWEST TOTAL

101 v Surrey at Chelmsford
63 v Derbyshire at Chesterfield.

CENTURY PARTNERSHIPS (11)

219	4th wkt	K.S. McEwan & K.W.R. Fletcher	v	Warwickshire at Edgbaston, Birmingham
176	4th wkt	K.S. McEwan & K.W.R. Fletcher	v	Yorkshire at Scarborough
170	1st wkt	M.H. Denness & G.A. Gooch	v	Sussex at Southend
148	3rd wkt	G.A. Gooch & K.W.R. Fletcher	v	Derbyshire at Chesterfield
141*	2nd wkt	G.A. Gooch & K.S. McEwan	v	Glamorgan at Ilford
131	3rd wkt	M.H. Denness & K.S. McEwan	v	Derbyshire at Chelmsford
114	8th wkt	B.R. Hardie & R.E. East	v	Hampshire at Bournemouth
113	1st wkt	M.H. Denness & B.R. Hardie	v	Northamptonshire at Northampton
111	1st wkt	M.H. Denness & G.A. Gooch	v	Yorkshire at Scarborough
110	4th wkt	K.W.R. Fletcher & B.R. Hardie	v	Derbyshire at Chesterfield
100	7th wkt	S. Turner & N. Phillip	v	Kent at Chelmsford

CENTURY PARTNERSHIPS BY OPPONENTS (6)

186*	2nd wkt	J.F. Steele & J.C. Balderstone	for Leicestershire at Leicester
140	6th wkt	C.H. Dredge & V.J. Marks	for Somerset at Bath
118	3rd wkt	R.G. Lumb & P. Carrick	for Yorkshire at Scarborough
117	1st wkt	C.G. Greenidge & J.M. Rice	for Hampshire at Bournemouth
113	3rd wkt	C.J. Tavare & C.S. Cowdrey	for Kent at Tunbridge Wells
113	3rd wkt	G.P. Howarth & R.D.V. Knight	for Surrey at Chelmsford

CENTURIES (11)

K.S. McEwan (3)	208*	v	Warwickshire at Edgbaston, Birmingham
	185	v	Derbyshire at Chelmsford
	124	v	Yorkshire at Scarborough
B.R. Hardie (3)	146*	v	Hampshire at Bournemouth
	103*	v	Northamptonshire at Northampton
	100*	v	Lancashire at Ilford

M.H. Denness (2)	136	v	Sussex at Southend
	122	v	Leicestershire at Chelmsford
K.W.R. Fletcher (1)	140*	v	Derbyshire at Chesterfield
G.A. Gooch (1)	109	v	Derbyshire at Chesterfield
S. Turner (1)	102	v	Kent at Chelmsford

CENTURIES BY OPPONENTS (8)

C.J. Tavare	150*	for Kent at Tunbridge Wells
J.A. Ormrod	134	for Worcestershire at Worcester
P. Willey	131	for Northamptonshire at Northampton
Yashpal Sharma	111	for India at Chelmsford
R.G. Lumb	110	for Yorkshire at Scarborough
C.J.C. Rowe	108*	for Kent at Chelmsford
J.F. Steele	107*	for Leicestershire at Leicester
G.P. Howarth	103	for Surrey at Chelmsford

FIFTIES

For   36   Against   30

FIVE OR MORE WICKETS IN AN INNINGS (18)

J.K. Lever (8)	8 for 49)		
	5 for 38)	v	Warwickshire at Edgbaston, Birmingham
	7 for 27	v	Lancashire at Ilford
	7 for 40	v	Hampshire at Bournemouth
	6 for 76)		
	7 for 41)	v	Leicestershire at Chelmsford
	6 for 52	v	Derbyshire at Chesterfield
	5 for 72	v	Derbyshire at Chelmsford
S. Turner (4)	5 for 35	v	Yorkshire at Scarborough
	5 for 39	v	Northamptonshire at Chelmsford
	5 for 70)		
	5 for 56)	v	Northamptonshire at Northampton
D.L. Acfield (3)	6 for 56	v	Gloucestershire at Castle Park, Colchester
	5 for 28	v	Nottinghamshire at Southend
	5 for 61	v	Hampshire at Bournemouth
N. Phillip (1)	5 for 23	v	Derbyshire at Chesterfield
K.W.R. Fletcher (1)	5 for 41	v	Middlesex at Castle Park, Colchester
R.E. East (1)	5 for 56	v	Nottinghamshire at Southend

FIVE OR MORE WICKETS IN AN INNINGS BY OPPONENTS (13)

W.W. Daniel	6 for 38	for Middlesex at Castle Park, Colchester
N.G.B. Cook	6 for 57	for Leicestershire at Leicester
Sarfraz Nawaz	6 for 60	for Northamptonshire at Northampton
L.B. Taylor	6 for 61	for Leicestershire at Chelmsford
G.W. Johnson	5 for 12	for Kent at Chelmsford
H.R. Moseley	5 for 18	for Somerset at Bath
J. Cumbes	5 for 31	for Worcestershire at Worcester
B.M. Brain	5 for 33	for Gloucestershire at Castle Park, Colchester
J.D. Inchmore	5 for 34	for Worcestershire at Worcester
P. Carrick	5 for 61	for Yorkshire at Scarborough
K. Higgs	5 for 72	for Leicestershire at Chelmsford
B.J. Griffiths	5 for 76	for Northamptonshire at Chelmsford
M.K. Bore	5 for 79	for Nottinghamshire at Southend

CAREER FIGURES — FIRST-CLASS MATCHES FOR ESSEX

Batting

	Matches	Inns	NO	Runs	HS	Av	100s	50s	0s	1000s
D.L. Acfield (1966–79)	225	214	115	866	38	8.74	–	–	39	–
M.H. Denness (1977–79)	65	107	5	3245	195	31.81	6	15	6	2
R.E. East (1965–79)	319	411	96	5615	113	17.82	1	20	59	–
K.W.R. Fletcher (1962–79)	380	640	83	20882	228*	37.49	31	127	48	14
G.A. Gooch (1973–79)	107	174	16	5251	136	33.23	9	27	17	1
B.R. Hardie (1973–79)	134	225	28	6447	162	32.72	9	32	19	4
R. Herbert (1976–77)	3	5	0	33	12	6.60	–	–	1	–
J.K. Lever (1967–79)	259	269	124	1536	91	10.59	–	1	35	–
A.W. Lilley (1978–79)	5	7	1	198	100*	33.00	1	–	1	–
M.S.A. McEvoy (1976–79)	16	26	1	404	67*	16.16	–	3	5	–
K.S. McEwan (1974–79)	134	221	16	8806	218	42.95	26	38	15	6
S.J. Malone (1975–78)	2	–	–	–	–	–	–	–	–	–
N. Phillip (1978–79)	42	58	9	1070	134	21.83	1	5	7	–
K.R. Pont (1970–79)	114	179	24	3670	113	23.67	5	18	22	–
D.R. Pringle (1978)	3	5	1	60	50*	15.00	–	1	1	–
G.E. Sainsbury (1979)	1	–	–	–	–	–	–	–	–	–
G.J. Saville (1963–74)	124	214	29	4265	126*	23.05	2	21	19	1
N. Smith (1973–79)	147	189	38	2744	126	18.17	2	7	27	–
B. Taylor (1949–73)	539	901	69	18240	135	21.92	9	78	101	8
S. Turner (1965–79)	259	374	69	6617	121	21.69	4	26	40	–

Bowling and Fielding

	Overs	Mdns	Runs	Wkts	Av	5wI	10wM	Best	100w	Ct	St
D.L. Acfield	5954.3	1704	14072	524	26.85	18	2	7–36	–	75	–
M.H. Denness	1	1	0	0	–	–	–	–	–	31	–
R.E. East	8644	2569	20353	815	24.97	38	7	8–30	–	202	–
K.W.R. Fletcher	185.5	35	737	21	35.09	1	–	5–41	–	371	–
G.A. Gooch	370.1	79	1101	28	39.32	1	–	5–40	–	83	–
B.R. Hardie	8	0	60	2	30.00	–	–	2–39	–	128	–
R. Herbert	–	–	–	–	–	–	–	–	–	2	–
J.K. Lever	6912.4	1497	18287	796	22.97	37	3	8–49	2	109	–
A.W. Lilley	–	–	–	–	–	–	–	–	–	1	–
M.S.A. McEvoy	3	1	4	0	–	–	–	–	–	18	–
K.S. McEwan	16.2	2	87	2	43.50	–	–	1–0	–	98	–
S.J. Malone	41	7	101	2	50.50	–	–	1–28	–	–	–
N. Phillip	1131.2	242	3097	141	21.96	5	–	6–33	–	10	–
K.R. Pont	632	119	1877	56	33.51	–	–	4–100	–	62	–
D.R. Pringle	23	8	50	1	50.00	–	–	1–31	–	1	–
G.E. Sainsbury	23	2	79	1	79.00	–	–	1–38	–	1	–
G.J. Saville	15	4	59	3	19.66	–	–	2–30	–	101	–
N. Smith	–	–	–	–	–	–	–	–	–	319	41
B. Taylor	8.3	2	21	1	21.00	–	–	1–16	–	1039	192
S. Turner	6631.3	1699	15661	630	24.85	23	1	6–26	–	176	–

FIRST-CLASS CAREER FIGURES TO END OF 1979 SEASON
(Where different from Essex figures)

Batting

	Matches	Inns	NO	Runs	HS	Av	100s	50s	0s	1000s
D.L. Acfield (1966–79)	267	278	136	1284	42	9.04	–	–	50	–
M.H. Denness (1959–79)	483	808	61	25081	195	33.57	33	144	53	15
R.E. East (1965–79)	323	413	97	5643	113	17.85	1	20	59	–
K.W.R. Fletcher (1962–79)	522	868	125	28521	228*	38.38	48	169	61	15
G.A. Gooch (1973–79)	135	220	19	6518	136	32.42	9	38	21	3
B.R. Hardie (1970–79)	138	232	29	6605	162	32.53	9	32	20	4
J.K. Lever (1967–79)	311	323	137	1996	91	10.73	–	2	39	–
K.S. McEwan (1972–79)	189	320	25	11305	218	38.32	27	52	23	6
N. Phillip (1970–79)	104	157	23	3440	134	25.67	1	21	16	–
D.R. Pringle (1978–79)	14	18	4	464	103*	33.14	1	3	2	–
G.J. Saville (1963–74)	126	218	29	4474	126*	23.67	3	22	19	1
N. Smith (1970–79)	156	202	44	2855	126	18.06	2	7	28	–
B. Taylor (1949–73)	572	949	73	19094	135	21.79	9	82	103	8
S. Turner (1965–79)	266	384	72	6764	121	21.67	4	26	40	–
Test Match Career Figures										
M.H. Denness (1969–75)	28	45	3	1667	188	39.69	4	7	2	
K.W.R. Fletcher (1968–77)	52	85	11	2975	216	40.20	7	16	6	
G.A. Gooch (1975–79)	17	27	2	754	91*	30.16	–	6	3	
J.K. Lever (1976–79)	15	22	4	229	53	12.72	–	1	1	
N. Phillip (1978–79)	9	15	5	297	47	29.70	–	–	1	

Bowling and Fielding

	Overs 6b	8b	Mdns	Runs	Wkts	Av	5wI	10wM	Best	100w	Ct	St
D.L. Acfield	7323	–	2148	17363	619	28.05	22	2	7–36	–	92	–
M.H. Denness	14	–	3	62	2	31.00	–	–	1–7	–	404	–
R.E. East	8750	–	2599	20639	823	25.07	38	7	8–30	–	204	–
K.W.R. Fletcher	328.5	46.3	56	1644	41	40.09	1	–	5–41	–	487	–
G.A. Gooch	425.1	26	93	1316	30	43.86	1	–	5–40	–	112	–
B.R. Hardie	8	–	0	60	2	30.00	–	–	2–39	–	131	–
J.K. Lever	7896.2	386.3	1798	22015	950	23.17	42	4	8–49	2	128	–
K.S. McEwan	16.2	–	2	87	2	43.50	–	–	1–0	–	194	8
N. Phillip	2709.4	5	580	7546	325	23.21	11	1	6–33	–	31	–
D.R. Pringle	282.3	–	87	660	23	28.69	–	–	4–43	–	8	–
G.J. Saville	17	–	4	76	3	25.33	–	–	2–30	–	103	–
N. Smith	–	–	–	–	–	–	–	–	–	–	333	45
B. Taylor	9.3	–	2	30	1	30.00	–	–	1–16	–	1082	212
S. Turner	6759.3	–	1725	16025	641	25.00	23	1	6–26	–	178	–

Test Match Career Figures

	Overs 6b	8b	Mdns	Runs	Wkts	Av	5wI	10wM	Best	100w	Ct	St
M.H. Denness	–	–	–	–	–	–	–	–	–	–	28	–
K.W.R. Fletcher	14	20.5	4	173	1	173.00	–	–	1–48		46	–
G.A. Gooch	35	6	10	93	1	93.00	–	–	1–16		20	–
J.K. Lever	258.3	166.7	88	1204	51	23.60	2	1	7–46		8	–
N. Phillip	306.2	–	46	1041	28	37.17	–	–	4–48		5	–

CAREER BEST PERFORMANCES 1979

K.W.R. Fletcher — Best bowling: 5–41 v Middlesex at Castle Park, Colchester

B.R. Hardie — Best bowling: 2–39 v Glamorgan at Ilford

J.K. Lever — Best bowling: 8–49 (13–87 in match) v Warwickshire at Edgbaston, Birmingham

N. Phillip — Highest Test score: 47 for West Indies v India at Calcutta
Best Test bowling: 4–48 (7–85 in match) for West Indies v India at Madras

S. Turner — Best match analysis: 10–126 v Northamptonshire at Northampton

The following bowlers had their most successful season:

K.W.R. Fletcher — 9 wickets (av 14.88)

B.R. Hardie — 2 wickets (av 19.50)

J.K. Lever — Took 106 wickets for the second time, equalling his total for 1978

The following fielders had their most successful season:

G.A. Gooch — 28 catches

B.R. Hardie — 30 catches

M.S.A. McEvoy — 11 catches

N. Phillip — 6 catches

The Benson and Hedges Cup
Competition

v NORTHAMPTONSHIRE AT NORTHAMPTON
5 May

Essex

A.W. Lilley	lbw, b Willey	27
G.A. Gooch	c Cook, b Sarfraz	83
K.S. McEwan	c Watts, b Larkins	3
K.W.R. Fletcher	b Sarfraz	65
B.R. Hardie	b Griffiths	35
K.R Pont	not out	3
S. Turner	not out	3
	b 6, nb 4, w 1	11
	for 5 wickets	230

	O	M	R	W
Sarfraz	11	3	41	2
Griffiths	10	4	58	1
T.M. Lamb	10	2	32	—
Watts	4	—	20	—
Willey	11	—	37	1
Larkins	8	1	31	1

fall of wickets
1–67, 2– 70, 3– 166, 4– 218, 5– 226

Northamptonshire

G. Cook	c Gooch, b Acfield	40
W. Larkins	c Gooch, b Acfield	44
P. Willey	b Pont	8
A.J. Lamb	c Pont, b Lever	77
T.J. Yardley	b Phillip	33
†P.J. Watts	lbw, b Phillip	0
*G. Sharp	b Lever	5
R.G. Williams	not out	5
Sarfraz Nawaz	not out	2
	lb 13	13
	for 7 wickets	227

	O	M	R	W
Lever	11	1	63	2
Phillip	11	–	32	2
Acfield	11	1	34	2
Turner	11	1	48	–
Pont	11	1	37	1

fall of wickets
1– 85, 2– 88, 3– 118, 4– 197, 5– 197, 6– 217, 7– 225

N. Phillip, *N. Smith, J.K. Lever and D. Acfield (Essex) and T.M. Lamb and B.J. Griffiths (Northamptonshire) did not bat.

Umpires – B. Meyer and C.T. Spencer

Essex won by 3 runs

Northamptonshire won the toss and asked Essex to bat

v SURREY AT THE OVAL
12 May

Surrey

A.R. Butcher	c Smith, b Turner	13
G.S. Clinton	c Gooch, b Acfield	18
G.P. Howarth	b Lever	75
†R.D.V. Knight	c Acfield, b Lever	52
D.M. Smith	b Lever	4
G.R.J. Roope	not out	26
R.D. Jackman	b Lever	1
S.T. Clarke	not out	2
	b 1, lb 14, nb 1	16
	for 6 wickets	207

	O	M	R	W
Lever	11	1	29	4
Phillip	11	1	49	–
Turner	11	3	40	1
Pont	11	2	39	–
Acfield	11	3	34	1

fall of wickets
1– 22, 2– 55, 3– 160, 4– 168, 5– 185, 6– 187

Essex

G.A. Gooch	c Roope, b Jackman	2
A.W. Lilley	b Clarke	33
K.S. McEwan	b Wilson	6
K.W.R. Fletcher	b Jackman	72
B.R. Hardie	b Clarke	0
K.R. Pont	b Wilson	32
S. Turner	b Wilson	0
N. Phillip	c Clinton, b Clarke	14
*N. Smith	c Wilson, b Clarke	10
J.K. Lever	b Jackman	9
D.L. Acfield	not out	1
	b 1, lb 11, w 1, nb 8	21
		200

	O	M	R	W
Clarke	10.4	3	23	4
Jackman	11	1	37	3
Wilson	11	—	38	3
Smith	11	1	47	—
Pocock	11	2	34	—

fall of wickets
1– 3, 2– 18, 3– 66, 4– 66, 5– 156, 6– 156, 7– 170, 8– 180, 9– 198

*C.J. Richards, P.I. Pocock and P.H.L. Wilson (Surrey) did not bat

Umpires — W.L. Budd and W.J. Dennis

Surrey won by 7 runs
Surrey won the toss

v COMBINED UNIVERSITIES AT CHELMSFORD
19 May

Essex

G.A. Gooch	c Mubarak, b Cooper	133
A.W. Lilley	c L'Estrange, b Greig	119
K.S. McEwan	b Pringle	44
K.W.R. Fletcher	not out	21
B.R. Hardie	not out	15
	b 2, lb 10, w 6	18
	for 3 wickets	350

	O	M	R	W
Ameer Hameed	11	2	41	—
Knight	7	—	37	—
Pringle	11	—	74	1
Ross	9	—	75	—
Cooper	7	—	48	1
Greig	10	—	57	1

fall of wickets
1– 223, 2– 305, 3– 320

Combined Universities

N.H.C. Cooper	c McEwan, b Lever	1
A.M. Mubarak	b Turner	30
S.M. Clements	c sub (East), b Lever	4
N. Gandon	b Phillip	1
M. L'Estrange	b Lever	1
D.R. Pringle	b Acfield	58
†I.A. Greig	c Smith, b Lever	3
Ameer Hameed	b Turner	16
*S.M. Skala	lbw, b Turner	0
J. Knight	b Acfield	4
C.J. Ross	not out	2
	b 1, lb 10, w 4, nb 1	16
		136

	O	M	R	W
Lever	11	4	18	4
Phillip	10	–	50	1
Turner	11	1	33	2
Acfield	5.3	1	14	2
Gooch	2	1	5	–

fall of wickets
1– 12, 2– 18, 3– 20, 4– 38, 5– 48, 6– 51, 7– 93, 8– 93, 9– 98

*N. Smith, K.R. Pont, S. Turner, N. Phillip, J.K. Lever and D.L. Acfield (Essex) did not bat

Umpires – P.B. Wight and J.G. Langridge

Essex won by 214 runs

Combined Universities won the toss and asked Essex to bat

v SUSSEX AT CHELMSFORD
23 May

Sussex

J.R.T. Barclay	c Smith, b Lever	19
G.D. Mendis	b Turner	15
P.W.G. Parker	c Gooch, b Pont	5
Javed Miandad	c Acfield, b Turner	47
Imran Khan	c Fletcher, b Phillip	20
P.J. Graves	b Lever	18
C.P. Phillipson	not out	38
R.G.L. Cheatle	c Fletcher, b Lever	8
†*A. Long	b Phillip	3
G.G. Arnold	not out	2
	b 4, lb 8, w 1	13
	for 8 wickets	188

	O	M	R	W
Lever	11	1	33	3
Phillip	11	1	42	2
Turner	11	2	16	2
Pont	11	—	54	1
Acfield	11	3	30	—

fall of wickets
1— 36, 2— 41, 3— 46, 4— 98, 5— 130, 6— 141, 7— 163, 8— 170

Essex

G.A. Gooch	c Mendis, b Spencer	66
A.W. Lilley	c Mendis, b Cheatle	70
K.S. McEwan	c Imran, b Spencer	44
K.W.R. Fletcher	not out	6
B.R. Hardie	not out	0
	w 2, nb 1	3
	for 3 wickets	189

	O	M	R	W
Imran	7	2	17	—
Arnold	11	2	22	—
Spencer	6.5	—	58	2
Cheatle	11	—	48	1
Phillipson	2	—	18	—
Barclay	3	—	23	—

fall of wickets
1— 108, 2— 169, 3— 187

J. Spencer (Sussex) and S. Turner, K.R. Pont, N. Phillip, *N. Smith, J.K. Lever and D.L. Acfield (Essex) did not bat

Umpires — R. Julian and A.G.T. Whitehead

Essex won by 7 wickets
Sussex won the toss

QUARTER-FINAL
v WARWICKSHIRE AT CHELMSFORD
6 June

Essex

G.A. Gooch	lbw, b Willis	138
A.W. Lilley	c Amiss, b Ferreira	0
K.S. McEwan	c and b Oliver	50
K.W.R. Fletcher	c Willis, b Perryman	43
B.R. Hardie	c Abberley, b Perryman	2
K.R. Pont	not out	22
N. Phillip	not out	7
	b 1, lb 6, w 2	9
	for 5 wickets	271

	O	M	R	W
Willis	11	5	32	1
Ferreira	11	2	72	1
Perryman	11	1	60	2
Oliver	11	—	52	1
Savage	11	—	46	—

fall of wickets
1– 2, 2– 107, 3– 197, 4– 218, 5– 263

Warwickshire

D.L. Amiss	c Smith, b Turner	17
K.D. Smith	c Gooch, b East	61
J. Whitehouse	run out	2
A.I. Kallicharran	c Smith, b Turner	2
P.R. Oliver	c Lilley, b East	46
*G.W. Humpage	c and b Pont	24
R.N. Abberley	b Lever	23
A.M. Ferreira	c East, b Lever	13
R.G.D. Willis	b Phillip	0
S.P. Perryman	b Phillip	18
R.L. Savage	not out	1
	b 1, lb 11, w 6, nb 2	20
		227

	O	M	R	W
Lever	10	—	41	2
Phillip	10.1	—	30	2
Turner	11	1	47	2
Pont	11	—	50	1
East	11	3	39	2

fall of wickets
1– 29, 2– 31, 3– 36, 4– 130, 5– 139, 6– 180, 7– 204, 8– 205, 9– 211

S. Turner, *N. Smith, R.E. East and J.K. Lever (Essex) did not bat

Umpires — R. Julian and K.E. Palmer

Essex won by 44 runs
Essex won the toss

SEMI-FINAL
v YORKSHIRE AT CHELMSFORD
4 July

Yorkshire

R.G. Lumb	b Phillip	75
†J.H. Hampshire	c Turner, b East	53
K. Sharp	lbw, b Phillip	0
C.W.J. Athey	b East	1
J.D. Love	c McEwan, b Pont	2
*D.L. Bairstow	run out	10
A. Sidebottom	c Fletcher, b Turner	0
P. Carrick	b Lever	1
G.B. Stevenson	b Lever	13
C.M. Old	not out	1
H.P. Cooper	not out	4
	lb 7, nb 6	13
	for 9 wickets	173

	O	M	R	W
Lever	11	2	31	2
Phillip	11	2	28	2
Turner	11	2	31	1
Pont	11	—	45	1
East	11	1	25	2

fall of wickets
1— 107, 2— 109, 3— 114, 4— 123, 5— 146, 6— 152, 7— 153, 8— 159, 9— 168

Essex

G.A. Gooch	c Bairstow, b Sidebottom	49
A.W. Lilley	c Bairstow, b Stevenson	0
K.S. McEwan	c Bairstow, b Sidebottom	18
K.W.R. Fletcher	c Sidebottom, b Stevenson	7
B.R. Hardie	c Bairstow, b Sidebottom	24
K.R. Pont	c Love, b Cooper	36
N. Phillip	c Sidebottom, b Carrick	9
S. Turner	not out	11
*N. Smith	not out	4
	b 4, lb 3, w 3, nb 6	16
	for 7 wickets	174

	O	M	R	W
Old	11	2	19	—
Stevenson	11	4	43	2
Sidebottom	11	1	35	3
Cooper	10	1	29	1
Carrick	11	—	32	1

fall of wickets
1— 2, 2— 42, 3— 68, 4— 99, 5— 112, 6— 139, 7— 169

R.E. East and J.K. Lever (Essex) did not bat

Umpires — D. Oslear and A.G.T. Whitehead

Essex won by 3 wickets
Essex won the toss and asked Yorkshire to bat

FINAL

v SURREY AT LORD'S
21 July

Essex

M.H. Denness	c Smith, b Wilson	24
G.A. Gooch	b Wilson	120
K.S. McEwan	c Richards, b Wilson	72
K.W.R. Fletcher|	b Knight	34
B.R. Hardie	c Intikhab, b Wilson	4
K.R. Pont	not out	19
N. Phillip	c Howarth, b Jackman	2
S. Turner	not out	1
	b 3, lb 8, w 1, nb 2	14
	for 6 wickets	290

	O	M	R	W
Jackman	11	–	69	1
Wilson	11	1	56	4
Knight	11	1	40	1
Intikhab	11	–	38	–
Pocock	11	–	73	–

fall of wickets
1– 48, 2– 172, 3– 239, 4– 261, 5– 273, 6– 276

Surrey

A.R. Butcher	c Smith, b Lever	13
M.A. Lynch	c McEwan, b East	17
G.P. Howarth	c Fletcher, b Pont	74
R.D.V. Knight	c Smith, b Pont	52
D.M. Smith	b Phillip	24
G.R.J. Roope	not out	39
Intikhab Alam	c Pont, b Phillip	1
R.D. Jackman	b East	1
*C.J. Richards	b Turner	1
P.I. Pocock	b Phillip	7
P.H.L. Wilson	b Lever	0
	b 4, lb 16, w 1, nb 5	26
		255

	O	M	R	W
Lever	9.4	2	33	2
Phillip	10	–	42	3
East	11	1	40	2
Turner	11	1	47	1
Pont	10	–	67	2

fall of wickets
1– 21, 2– 45, 3– 134, 4– 187, 5– 205, 6– 219, 7– 220, 8– 226, 9– 250

*N. Smith, R.E. East and J.K. Lever (Essex) did not bat

Umpires — H.D. Bird and B.J. Meyer

Essex won by 35 runs
Surrey won the toss and asked Essex to bat

Essex in the Benson and Hedges Cup 1979

Played 7; won 6; lost 1.
Position in Group "C" Zonal Table: Equal first with Surrey.
Cup winners, defeating Surrey in the Final at Lord's on 21st July 1979.

BATTING AVERAGES

Cap		Matches	Inns	NO	Runs	HS	Av	100s	50s	0s
1975	G.A. Gooch	7	7	0	591	138	84.42	3	2	—
1976	K.R. Pont	7	5	3	112	36	56.00	—	—	—
1963	K.W.R. Fletcher	7	7	2	248	72	49.60	—	2	—
—	A.W. Lilley	6	6	0	249	119	41.50	1	1	2
1974	K.S. McEwan	7	7	0	237	72	33.85	—	—	—
1977	M.H. Denness	1	1	0	24	24	24.00	—	—	—
1974	B.R. Hardie	7	7	2	80	35	16.00	—	—	1
1970	S. Turner	7	4	3	15	11*	15.00	—	—	1
1975	N. Smith	7	2	1	14	10	14.00	—	—	—
1978	N. Phillip	7	4	1	32	14	10.66	—	—	—
1970	J.K. Lever	7	1	0	9	9	9.00	—	—	—
1970	D.L. Acfield	4	1	1	1	1*	—	—	—	—
1967	R.E. East	3	—	—	—	—	—	—	—	—

Runs		1612
Byes		11
Leg byes		43
Wides		16
No balls		22

	Matches	Inns	NO	Runs	HS	Av	100s	50s	0s
TOTALS	7	52	13	1704	138	43.69	4	7	4

Mode of Dismissal

	Bowled	C & B	Caught	Caught WK	Lbw	Total
Gooch	1	—	4	1	1	7
Pont	1	—	1	—	—	2
Fletcher	3	—	2	—	—	5
Lilley	1	—	3	1	1	6
McEwan	2	1	2	2	—	7
Denness	—	—	1	—	—	1
Hardie	2	—	2	1	—	5
Turner	1	—	—	—	—	1
Smith	—	—	1	—	—	1
Phillip	—	—	3	—	—	3
Lever	1	—	—	—	—	1
Totals	12	1	19	5	2	39

Scoring Rate
Runs scored from 2199 balls at a rate of 77.49 per 100 balls or 4.649 per over.

Striking Rate
Opponents took wickets at a rate of 56.38 balls per wicket.

BOWLING AVERAGES

	Type	M	I	O	Mdns	R	W	Av	4wI	Best
J.K. Lever	LFM	7	7	74.4	13	248	19	13.05	2	4—18
R.E. East	SLA	3	3	33	5	104	6	17.33	—	2—25
D.L. Acfield	OB	4	4	38.3	8	112	5	22.40	—	2—14
N. Phillip	RFM	7	7	75.1	6	273	12	22.75	—	3—42
S. Turner	RFM	7	7	77	11	262	10	26.20	—	3—33
K.R. Pont	RM	7	6	65	4	292	6	48.66	—	2—67
G.A. Gooch	RM	7	1	2	1	5	0	—	—	—
Runs						1296	58	22.34		
Byes						11				
Leg byes						79				
Wides						12				
No balls						15				
Run outs							2			
TOTALS		7	7	365.2	48	1413	60	23.55	2	4—18

Mode of Dismissal

	Bowled	C & B	Caught	Caught sub	Caught WK	Lbw	Total	Run Out
Lever	10	—	5	1	3	—	19	
East	2	—	4	—	—	—	6	
Acfield	2	—	3	—	—	—	5	
Phillip	8	—	2	—	—	2	12	
Turner	4	—	2	—	3	1	10	
Pont	1	1	3	—	1	—	6	
Totals	27	1	19	1	7	3	58	2

Scoring Rate
Opponents scored their runs from 2192 balls at a rate of 64.46 per 100 balls or 3.868 per over.

Striking Rate
Wickets were taken at a rate of 36.53 balls per wicket.

CATCHES

N. Smith	7
G.A. Gooch	5
K.W.R. Fletcher	4
K.S. McEwan, K.R. Pont	3 each
D.L. Acfield	2
R.E. East, A.W. Lilley, S. Turner, Substitute (R.E. East)	1 each

HIGHEST TOTAL	LOWEST TOTAL

For: 350—3 in 55 overs v Combined   200 v Surrey at The Oval
                  Universities at Chelmsford
                  (Benson & Hedges Cup record highest total)
Against: 255 v Surrey at Lord's   136 v Combined Universities at
                                            Chelmsford

CENTURY PARTNERSHIPS (4)

223	1st wkt	G.A. Gooch & A.W. Lilley	v Combined Universities at Chelmsford
		(Benson & Hedges Cup record)	
124	2nd wkt	G.A. Gooch & K.S. McEwan	v Surrey at Lord's
108	1st wkt	G.A. Gooch & A.W. Lilley	v Sussex at Chelmsford
105	2nd wkt	G.A. Gooch & K.S. McEwan	v Warwickshire at Chelmsford

CENTURY PARTNERSHIPS BY OPPONENTS (2)

107	1st wkt	J.H. Hampshire & R.G. Lumb	for Yorkshire at Chelmsford
105	3rd wkt	G.P. Howarth & R.D.V. Knight	for Surrey at The Oval

CENTURIES (4)

G.A. Gooch (3)	138	v Warwickshire at Chelmsford
	133	v Combined Universities at Chelmsford
	120	v Surrey at Lord's
A.W. Lilley (1)	119	v Combined Universities at Chelmsford

FIFTIES

For	7	Against	9

FOUR OR MORE WICKETS IN AN INNINGS (2)

J.K. Lever (2)	4 for 18	v Combined Universities at Chelmsford
	4 for 29	v Surrey at The Oval

FOUR OR MORE WICKETS IN AN INNINGS BY OPPONENTS (2)

S.T. Clarke	4 for 23	for Surrey at The Oval
P.H.L. Wilson	4 for 56	for Surrey at Lord's

CAREER FIGURES – BENSON AND HEDGES CUP MATCHES FOR ESSEX

Batting

	Matches	Inns	NO	Runs	HS	Av	100s	50s	0s
D.L. Acfield (1972–79)	14	3	2	10	6*	10.00	–	–	–
M.H. Denness (1977–79)	9	8	1	187	53	26.71	–	1	1
R.E. East (1972–79)	34	20	9	218	54	19.81	–	1	2
K.W.R. Fletcher (1972–79)	37	36	4	869	90	27.15	–	6	3
G.A. Gooch (1973–79)	26	26	1	1025	138	41.00	3	6	2
B.R. Hardie (1974–79)	27	27	5	441	42*	20.04	–	–	2
J.K. Lever (1972–79)	39	14	10	66	12*	16.50	–	–	–
A.W. Lilley (1979)	6	6	0	249	119	41.50	1	1	2
K.S. McEwan (1974–79)	29	28	0	1035	133	36.96	2	6	1
N. Phillip (1978–79)	8	5	2	40	14	13.33	–	–	–
K.R. Pont (1972–79)	33	25	8	432	60*	25.41	–	1	3
D.R. Pringle (1978)	1	1	0	9	9	9.00	–	–	–
G.J. Saville (1972–73)	5	4	1	148	85*	49.33	–	1	1
N. Smith (1974–79)	29	16	3	154	61	11.84	–	1	–
B. Taylor (1972–73)	10	7	0	76	30	10.85	–	–	–
S. Turner (1972–79)	39	32	12	395	41*	19.75	–	–	4

Career Figures (where different from Essex figures)

	Matches	Inns	NO	Runs	HS	Av	100s	50s	0s
M.H. Denness (1972–79)	33	31	3	763	112*	27.25	2	3	7
D.R. Pringle (1978–79)	5	5	0	140	58	28.00	–	2	–

Bowling and Fielding

	Overs	Mdns	Runs	Wkts	Av	4wI	Best	Runs p over	Balls p wkt	Ct	St
D.L. Acfield	95	11	336	11	30.54	–	2–14	3.54	51.82	2	–
M.H. Denness	–	–	–	–	–	–	–	–	–	2	–
R.E. East	269	51	773	34	22.73	3	5–33	2.87	47.47	9	–
K.W.R. Fletcher	4	0	25	1	25.00	–	1–25	6.25	24.00	9	–
G.A. Gooch	78.3	10	293	8	36.62	–	2–36	3.73	58.87	12	–
B.R. Hardie	–	–	–	–	–	–	–	–	–	2	–
J.K. Lever	397.4	78	1148	69	16.63	5	5–16	2.89	34.58	8	–
A.W. Lilley	–	–	–	–	–	–	–	–	–	1	–
K.S. McEwan	–	–	–	–	–	–	–	–	–	7	–
N. Phillip	86.1	7	318	12	26.50	–	3–42	3.69	43.08	–	–
K.R. Pont	142	12	575	15	38.33	–	2–20	4.05	56.80	10	–
D.R. Pringle	8	1	30	0	–	–	–	3.75	–	–	–
G.J. Saville	–	–	–	–	–	–	–	–	–	3	–
N. Smith	–	–	–	–	–	–	–	–	–	24	2
B. Taylor	–	–	–	–	–	–	–	–	–	11	–
S. Turner	392.5	67	1122	56	20.03	1	4–22	2.86	42.09	11	–

Career Figures (where different from Essex figures)

	Overs	Mdns	Runs	Wkts	Av	4wI	Best	Runs p over	Balls p wkt	Ct	St
M.H. Denness	–	–	–	–	–	–	–	–	–	11	–
D.R. Pringle	38.4	1	195	2	97.50	–	1–59	5.04	116.00	2	–

CAREER BEST PERFORMANCES 1979

D.L. Acfield   Best bowling: 2—14 v Combined Universities at Chelmsford
G.A. Gooch   Highest score and highest for Essex in the competition: 138
                  v Warwickshire at Chelmsford
A.W. Lilley   Highest score: 119 v Combined Universities at Chelmsford
N. Phillip   Highest score: 14 v Surrey at The Oval
                  Best bowling: 3—42 v Surrey at Lord's

Gooch and McEwan both reached their thousand runs in the competition in the course of the Final at Lord's

Essex batsmen made the following record wicket partnerships:

223	1st wkt	G.A. Gooch & A.W. Lilley	v Combined Universities at Chelmsford
96	3rd wkt	G.A. Gooch & K.W.R. Fletcher	v Northamptonshire at Northampton
90	5th wkt	K.W.R. Fletcher & K.R. Pont	v Surrey at The Oval

Opponents made the following record wicket partnerships:

| 24 | 9th wkt | G.R.J. Roope & P.I. Pocock | for Surrey at Lord's |
| 38 | 10th wkt | D.R. Pringle & C.J. Ross | for Combined Universities at Chelmsford |

John Player League

The match v Nottinghamshire, 20 May, was abandoned without a ball
being bowled

v WARWICKSHIRE AT EDGBASTON
29 April

Essex

G.A. Gooch	c Humpage, b Perryman	33
A.W. Lilley	b Brown	17
K.S. McEwan	lbw, b Oliver	11
K.W.R. Fletcher	c Oliver, b Perryman	11
B.R. Hardie	b Brown	48
K.R. Pont	c Amiss, b Brown	29
S. Turner	b Brown	9
N. Smith	not out	2
R.E. East	b Brown	0

J.K. Lever and D.L. Acfield did not bat

	b 2, lb 12	14
	for 8 wkts	174

	O	M	R	W
Willis	8	—	40	—
Brown	8	—	22	5
Oliver	8	1	32	1
Ferreira	8	—	25	—
Perryman	8	—	41	2

fall of wickets
1– 28, 2– 55, 3– 71, 4– 87, 5– 156, 6– 172, 7– 174, 8– 174

Warwickshire

D.L. Amiss	st Smith, b East	35
K.D. Smith	b East	23
R.N. Abberley	b Pont	11
†J. Whitehouse	c Gooch, b Pont	11
*C. Maynard	b Lever	35
G.W. Humpage	b East	1
P.R. Oliver	c Turner, b Acfield	16
A. Ferreira	run out	12
D.J. Brown	b Pont	5
R.G.D. Willis	b Lever	0
S.P. Perryman	not out	0
	lb 10	10
		159

	O	M	R	W
Lever	8	1	15	2
Turner	8	1	34	–
East	8	3	20	3
Acfield	8	–	30	1
Gooch	1	–	9	–
Pont	6.2	–	41	3

fall of wickets
1– 47, 2– 51, 3– 64, 4– 88, 5– 90, 6– 132, 7– 143, 8– 154, 9– 157

Umpires – C. Cook and B.J. Meyer

Essex won by 15 runs
Essex won the toss

v DERBYSHIRE AT CHELMSFORD
6 May

Derbyshire
A.J. Borrington	c Acfield, b Pont	33
J.G. Wright	c Gooch, b Turner	10
P.N. Kirsten	c Turner, b Pont	23
K.J. Barnett	b Pont	13
J. Walters	st Smith, b Pont	2
†D.S. Steele	b Phillip	4
G. Miller	c Pont, b Lever	1
*R.W. Taylor	b Phillip	3
C.J. Tunnicliffe	c Hardie, b Lever	7
P.E. Russell	not out	2
M. Hendrick	c Hardie, b Phillip	2
	b 1, lb 13	14
		114

	O	M	R	W
Lever	8	2	12	2
Phillip	8	–	20	3
Acfield	8	1	17	–
Turner	8	1	27	1
Pont	8	2	24	4

fall of wickets
1– 26, 2– 72, 3– 81, 4– 89, 5– 92, 6– 97, 7– 97, 8– 106, 9– 108

Essex
G.A. Gooch	not out	68
A.W. Lilley	c Taylor, b Tunnicliffe	3
K.S. McEwan	c Steele, b Miller	22
K.W.R. Fletcher	not out	20

B.R. Hardie, K.R. Pont, S. Turner, N. Phillip, N. Smith,
J.K. Lever and D.L. Acfield did not bat

	lb 1, w 2, nb 2	5
	for 2 wkts	118

	O	M	R	W
Hendrick	8	1	12	–
Tunnicliffe	7	2	16	1
Miller	6	–	30	1
Russell	8	1	26	–
Kirsten	2	1	5	–
Walters	3.5	–	24	–

fall of wickets
1– 10, 2– 53

Umpires – D.J. Dennis and R. Julian

Essex won by 8 wickets
Derbyshire won the toss

v HAMPSHIRE AT SOUTHAMPTON
13 May

Essex

G.A. Gooch	c Stephenson, b Rice	25
A.W. Lilley	c Turner, b Stevenson	11
K.S. McEwan	c Stephenson, b Stevenson	5
K.W.R. Fletcher	b Tremlett	46
B.R. Hardie	run out	8
K.R. Pont	run out	38
N. Phillip	not out	15
S. Turner	not out	17

N. Smith, J.K. Lever and D.L. Acfield did not bat

	b 2, lb 5	7
	for 6 wkts	172

	O	M	R	W
Marshall	8	1	26	–
Stevenson	8	–	30	2
Tremlett	8	1	32	1
Rice	8	1	44	1
Taylor	8	–	33	–

fall of wickets
1– 22, 2– 42, 3– 50, 4– 67, 5– 128, 6– 142

Hampshire

C.G. Greenidge	b Lever	75
J.M. Rice	b Lever	0
D.R. Turner	b Lever	60
T.E. Jesty	not out	22
N.E.J. Pocock	not out	7

N.G. Cowley, M.N.S. Taylor, M.D. Marshall, †*G.R. Stephenson, T.M. Tremlett
and K. Stevenson did not bat

	b 2, lb 6, nb 1	9
	for 3 wkts	173

	O	M	R	W
Lever	8	1	24	3
Phillip	7	–	33	–
Acfield	8	1	31	–
Turner	8	–	28	–
Pont	7.1	–	48	–

fall of wickets
1– 1, 2– 136, 3– 147

Umpires – D.J. Constant and C.T. Spencer

Hampshire won by 7 wickets
Essex won the toss

v SURREY AT THE OVAL
27 May

Surrey

A.R. Butcher	c Pont, b Phillip	5
G.P. Howarth	c Acfield, b Phillip	3
G.R.J. Roope	c McEwan, b Phillip	0
†R.D.V. Knight	b Acfield	5
D.M. Smith	b Phillip	39
M.A. Lynch	c Hardie, b Turner	2
R.D. Jackman	c McEwan, b Pont	3
*C.J. Richards	c Lilley, b Turner	8
S.T. Clarke	lbw, b Lever	1
P.I. Pocock	not out	1
P.H.L. Wilson	b Lever	10
	lb 6, w 3, nb 2	11
		88

	O	M	R	W
Lever	7.2	2	9	2
Phillip	8	–	26	4
Acfield	8	3	12	1
Turner	8	2	14	2
Pont	7	2	16	1

fall of wickets
1– 5, 2– 5, 3– 8, 4– 18, 5– 27, 6– 43, 7– 64, 8– 71, 9– 76

Essex

G.A. Gooch	c Richards, b Clarke	11
A.W. Lilley	not out	6
K.S. McEwan	not out	4

K.W.R. Fletcher, B.R. Hardie, K.R. Pont, N. Phillip, S. Turner, N. Smith,
J.K. Lever and D.L. Acfield did not bat

	w 3	3
	for 1 wkt	24

	O	M	R	W
Clarke	5	3	10	1
Jackman	4.4	–	11	–

fall of wicket
1– 21

Umpires – D.J. Halfyard and D.G.L. Evans

Match abandoned as a draw
Essex won the toss and asked Surrey to bat

v LANCASHIRE AT ILFORD
3 June

Essex

G.A. Gooch	c Wood, b Hogg	0
A.W. Lilley	c Lyon, b Hogg	10
K.S. McEwan	b Hogg	5
K.W.R. Fletcher	c Wood, b Simmons	27
B.R. Hardie	b Lee	35
K.R. Pont	c Hughes, b Simmons	9
S. Turner	c Hogg, b Wood	6
N. Phillip	b Wood	2
N. Smith	not out	23
J.K. Lever	c Lyon, b Hogg	1
D.L. Acfield	not out	3
	b 3, w 3	6
	for 9 wkts	127

	O	M	R	W
Hogg	8	1	23	4
Lee	8	1	23	1
Wood	8	–	25	2
Reidy	8	–	31	–
Simmons	8	1	19	2

fall of wickets
1– 0, 2– 15, 3– 16, 4– 66, 5– 78, 6– 95, 7– 98, 8– 107, 9– 120

Lancashire

A. Kennedy	b Pont	12
B. Wood	b Lever	0
D. Lloyd	c McEwan, b Acfield	35
†F.C. Hayes	c Lilley, b Turner	24
C.H. Lloyd	not out	23
B.W. Reidy	not out	30

J. Simmons, *J. Lyon, P.G. Lee, D.P. Hughes and W. Hogg did not bat

	b 2, lb 2, nb 2	6
	for 4 wkts	130

	O	M	R	W
Lever	7.5	3	23	1
Phillip	6	1	29	–
Turner	8	3	20	1
Pont	7	3	16	1
Acfield	8	1	36	1

fall of wickets
1– 1, 2– 16, 3– 72, 4– 88

Umpires – C. Cook and A. Jepson

Lancashire won by 6 wickets
Essex won the toss

v SOMERSET AT BATH
17 June

Essex

M.H. Denness	c Denning, b Dredge	9
A.W. Lilley	b Breakwell	5
K.S. McEwan	b Breakwell	14
K.W.R. Fletcher	not out	51
B.R. Hardie	c Taylor, b Jennings	9
K.R. Pont	b Moseley	1
S. Turner	b Jennings	2
N. Phillip	c Rose, b Dredge	6
N. Smith	b Dredge	0
J.K. Lever	run out	2
D.L. Acfield	not out	1
	b 6, lb 10, w 3, nb 1	20
	for 9 wkts	120

	O	M	R	W
Moseley	8	2	18	1
Dredge	8	1	21	3
Burgess	8	–	15	–
Breakwell	8	1	24	2
Jennings	8	1	22	2

fall of wickets
1– 18, 2– 29, 3– 35, 4– 75, 5– 76, 6– 85, 7– 85, 8– 107, 9– 107

Somerset

†B.C. Rose	not out	50
P.W. Denning	b Acfield	41
P.M. Roebuck	not out	4

M.J. Kitchen, V.J. Marks, G.I. Burgess, D. Breakwell, *D.J.S. Taylor,
C.H. Dredge, K.F. Jennings and H.R. Moseley did not bat

	b 12, lb 11, w 2, nb 1	26
	for 1 wkt	121

	O	M	R	W	
Lever	4	1	3	—	
Phillip	4	2	7	—	
Turner	8	1	30	—	
Pont	8	—	30	—	
Acfield	8	—	24	1	
Fletcher	0.1	—	1	—	

fall of wicket
1— 109

Umpires — J.V.C. Griffiths and R. Julian

Somerset won by 9 wickets
Essex won the toss

v KENT AT CHELMSFORD
1 July

Kent

R.A. Woolmer	lbw, b Lever	5
G.W. Johnson	lbw, b Phillip	5
C.J. Tavare	b Pont	21
Asif Iqbal	lbw, b Phillip	0
†A.G.E. Ealham	c Lever, b Pont	10
J.N. Shepherd	c East, b Gooch	7
C.S. Cowdrey	lbw, b Turner	8
*A.P.E. Knott	not out	29
R.W. Hills	c Turner, b Phillip	15
D.L. Underwood	b Lever	3
K.B.S. Jarvis	b Phillip	0
	lb 6, w 5, nb 3	14
		117

	O	M	R	W
Lever	8	3	27	2
Phillip	7.2	—	23	4
Turner	8	—	19	1
Pont	8	2	12	2
Gooch	8	—	22	1

fall of wickets
1— 12, 2— 16, 3— 16, 4— 43, 5— 53, 6— 66, 7— 77, 8— 110, 9— 116

Essex

G.A. Gooch	not out	48
A.W. Lilley	c Jarvis, b Woolmer	28
K.S. McEwan	not out	36

K.W.R. Fletcher, B.R. Hardie, K.R. Pont, N. Phillip, S. Turner, N. Smith,
R.E. East and J.K. Lever did not bat

	b 4, lb 4, w 1	9
	for 1 wkt	121

	O	M	R	W
Jarvis	4	–	18	–
Shepherd	4	–	19	–
Woolmer	8	–	30	1
Hills	5	–	24	–
Underwood	5	–	21	–

fall of wickets
1– 58

Umpires – W.L. Budd and D.J. Dennis

Essex won by 9 wickets
Essex won the toss and asked Kent to bat

v SUSSEX AT SOUTHEND
8 July

Essex

G.A. Gooch	b Spencer	77
A.W. Lilley	c Long, b Arnold	21
K.S. McEwan	c Miandad, b Barclay	22
K.W.R. Fletcher	not out	46
B.R. Hardie	c Imran, b Barclay	23
K.R. Pont	run out	0
N. Phillip	not out	2

N. Smith, S. Turner, R.E. East and J.K. Lever did not bat

lb 3, w 2, nb 3   8

for 5 wkts   199

	O	M	R	W
Imran Khan	8	2	31	–
Spencer	7	–	45	1
Pigott	8	–	32	–
Arnold	8	–	30	1
Phillipson	4	–	29	–
Barclay	4	–	24	2

fall of wickets
1– 43, 2– 104, 3– 150, 4– 193, 5– 193

Sussex

G.D. Mendis	lbw, b Pont	49
P.J. Graves	c Smith, b East	55
Javed Miandad	c and b Pont	3
P.W.G. Parker	c Turner, b Phillip	20
Imran Khan	c East, b Lever	9
C.P. Phillipson	lbw, b Lever	2
J.R.T. Barclay	c Lilley, b Phillip	3
A.C.S. Pigott	not out	20
†A. Long	not out	17

J. Spencer and G.G. Arnold did not bat

lb 6, w 6   12

for 7 wkts   190

	O	M	R	W
Lever	8	—	33	2
Phillip	8	—	38	2
Turner	7	—	32	—
Pont	8	1	40	2
East	8	—	35	1

fall of wickets
1– 108, 2– 111, 3– 118, 4– 140, 5– 143, 6– 148, 7– 153

Umpires – K.E. Palmer and R. Herman

Essex won by 9 runs
Essex won the toss

v NORTHAMPTONSHIRE AT LUTON
15 July

Essex

M.H. Denness	lbw, b T. Lamb	44
A.W. Lilley	c Willey, b Griffiths	19
K.S. McEwan	c A.J. Lamb, b T. Lamb	29
K.W.R. Fletcher	c Williams, b Willey	6
B.R. Hardie	c Sharp, b Willey	14
K.R. Pont	c A.J. Lamb, b Willey	19
N. Phillip	c Sharp, b T. Lamb	0
S. Turner	lbw, b Sarfraz	20
N. Smith	not out	3
R.E. East	b Sarfraz	0
J.K. Lever	b Griffiths	0
	b 1, w 3, nb 6	10
		164

	O	M	R	W
Sarfraz Nawaz	6	—	20	2
Griffiths	5.4	—	36	2
Hodgson	8	—	43	—
T.M. Lamb	8	—	32	3
Willey	8	1	23	3

fall of wickets
1– 36, 2– 95, 3– 104, 4– 113, 5– 123, 6– 124, 7– 158, 8– 163, 9– 163

Northamptonshire

P. Willey	c Hardie, b East	12
G. Cook	c Turner, b Lever	6
A.J. Lamb	not out	51
R.G. Williams	c McEwan, b East	16
T.J. Yardley	c and b Lever	42
†P.J. Watts	b Lever	2
*G. Sharp	not out	15

Sarfraz Nawaz, A. Hodgson, T.M. Lamb and B.J. Griffiths did not bat

	b 5, lb 10, w 3, nb 3	21
	for 5 wkts	165

	O	M	R	W
Lever	7.4	—	31	3
Phillip	7	1	22	—
Turner	8	—	22	—
East	8	1	26	2
Pont	8	1	43	—

fall of wickets
1— 13, 2— 28, 3— 62, 4— 141, 5— 143

Umpires — C. Cook and J.G. Langridge

Northamptonshire won by 5 wickets
Essex won the toss

v YORKSHIRE AT CASTLE PARK, COLCHESTER
22 July

Yorkshire

G. Boycott	c Smith, b Turner	16
C.W.J. Athey	st Smith, b East	45
K. Sharp	c Smith, b East	1
†C.M. Old	c Turner, b East	18
G.B. Stevenson	b East	13
C. Johnson	c Hardie, b East	6
J.D. Love	b Lever	10
*D.L. Bairstow	c Gooch, b Lever	9
P. Carrick	not out	10
H.P. Cooper	not out	5
S. Oldham		
	b 2, lb 5, w 1, nb 1	9
	for 8 wkts	142

	O	M	R	W
Lever	7	1	23	2
Phillip	7	—	24	—
Turner	8	—	31	1
Pont	4	—	12	—
East	8	2	20	5
Gooch	4	—	23	—

fall of wickets
1— 38, 2— 52, 3— 82, 4— 95, 5— 101, 6— 106, 7— 123, 8— 131

Essex

G.A. Gooch	lbw, b Stevenson	2
A.W. Lilley	run out	12
K.S. McEwan	b Old	4
K.W.R. Fletcher	b Stevenson	10
B.R. Hardie	b Old	34
K.R. Pont	c Boycott, b Oldham	3
N. Phillip	b Cooper	10
S. Turner	c and b Old	20
N. Smith	b Cooper	9
R.E. East	not out	10
J.K. Lever	c Bairstow, b Cooper	5
	lb 7, w 5, nb 2	14
		133

	O	M	R	W
Old	8	–	30	3
Stevenson	8	2	16	2
Oldham	8	1	28	1
Cooper	7.1	–	26	3
Carrick	6	–	19	–

fall of wickets
1– 3, 2– 11, 3– 28, 4– 39, 5– 56, 6– 76, 7– 108, 8– 109, 9– 125

Umpires – D.O. Oslear and C. Cook

Yorkshire won by 9 runs
Essex won the toss and asked Yorkshire to bat

v GLOUCESTERSHIRE AT CASTLE PARK, COLCHESTER
29 July

Gloucestershire

Sadiq Mohammad	c Pont, b Gooch	37
Zaheer Abbas	c East, b Pont	50
†M.J. Procter	b Pont	0
J.C. Foat	run out	5
A.J. Hignell	b Phillip	6
A.W. Stovold	run out	12
M.D. Partridge	not out	11
P. Bainbridge	not out	1

J.H. Childs, D.A. Graveney and *A.J. Brassington did not bat

	lb 4, w 1	5
	for 6 wkts	127

	O	M	R	W
Lever	5	–	24	–
Turner	4	–	26	–
Gooch	4	–	25	1
Pont	4	–	30	2
Phillip	4	–	17	1

fall of wickets
1– 83, 2– 89, 3– 94, 4– 97, 5– 112, 6– 122

Essex

G.A. Gooch	c Graveney, b Partridge	7
A.W. Lilley	c Hignell, b Bainbridge	6
K.S. McEwan	c Stovold, b Childs	14
K.W.R. Fletcher	st Brassington, b Graveney	13
B.R. Hardie	b Childs	16
K.R. Pont	not out	31
N. Phillip	c Brassington, b Graveney	7
S. Turner	c Hignell, b Childs	20
N. Smith	not out	8

R.E. East and J.K. Lever did not bat

	b 1, lb 4, nb 1	6
	for 7 wkts	128

192 *Summer of Success*

	O	M	R	W
Partridge	4	–	28	1
Procter	4.5	1	18	–
Bainbridge	4	–	19	1
Childs	4	–	24	3
Graveney	4	–	33	2

fall of wickets
1– 9, 2– 27, 3– 31, 4– 58, 5–66, 6– 75, 7– 106

Umpires – J.G. Langridge and D.O. Oslear

Essex won by 3 wickets   Essex won the toss and asked Gloucestershire to bat

v LEICESTERSHIRE AT LEICESTER
19 August

Essex

M.H. Denness	c Dudleston, b Higgs	15
A.W. Lilley	c Birkenshaw, b Higgs	1
K.S. McEwan	c and b Steele	45
K.W.R. Fletcher	lbw, b Higgs	0
B.R. Hardie	lbw, b Steele	29
K.R. Pont	b Taylor	35
S. Turner	c Booth, b Taylor	20
N. Phillip	b Taylor	4
N. Smith	b Clift	3
R.E. East	b Clift	0
J.K. Lever	not out	1
	lb 7, w 3, nb 1	11
		164

	O	M	R	W
Taylor	7.4	1	34	3
Higgs	8	2	17	3
Booth	5	–	37	–
Steele	8	–	29	2
Briers	4	–	12	–
Clift	6	–	24	2

fall of wickets
1– 6, 2– 23, 3– 23, 4– 85, 5– 107, 6– 150, 7– 159, 8– 162, 9– 162

Leicestershire

N.E. Briers	b Turner	12
J. Birkenshaw	c McEwan, b Lever	6
B. Dudleston	c Hardie, b Turner	8
B.F. Davison	b East	23
*R.W. Tolchard	lbw, b East	5
M. Schepens	b Turner	8
P.B. Clift	b Pont	4
J.F. Steele	b Lever	6
P. Booth	b Fletcher	6
†K. Higgs	c East, b Lever	3
L.B. Taylor	not out	1
	b 2, lb 11, w 9	22
		104

	O	M	R	W
Lever	8	3	10	3
Phillip	7	2	11	—
Turner	8	3	15	3
Pont	8	1	22	1
East	8	1	20	2
Fletcher	0.4	—	4	1

fall of wickets
1– 17, 2– 20, 3– 37, 4– 63, 5– 78, 6– 84, 7– 88, 8– 92, 9– 98

Umpires — A.G.T. Whitehead and D.J. Dennis

Essex won by 60 runs   Leicestershire won the toss and asked Essex to bat

v MIDDLESEX AT CHELMSFORD
26 August

Essex

G.A. Gooch	b Jones	10
A.W. Lilley	b Edmonds	28
K.S. McEwan	b Jones	2
K.W.R. Fletcher	st Gould, b Edmonds	46
B.R. Hardie	not out	55
K.R. Pont	st Gould, b Emburey	14
S. Turner	not out	19

N. Smith, N. Phillip, J.K. Lever and R.E. East did not bat

b 3, lb 9, w 3	15
for 5 wkts	189

	O	M	R	W
Selvey	8	—	29	—
Jones	8	2	15	2
Herkes	8	—	58	—
Emburey	5	—	37	1
Edmonds	8	2	20	2
Gatting	3	—	15	—

fall of wickets
1– 21, 2– 25, 3– 77, 4– 129, 5– 148

Middlesex

M.J. Smith	lbw, b Phillip	4
†C.T. Radley	c McEwan, b Pont	24
G.D. Barlow	lbw, b Turner	6
R.O. Butcher	b Turner	0
M.W. Gatting	c Gooch, b Turner	4
P.H. Edmonds	c McEwan, b East	3
*I.J. Gould	lbw, b Pont	0
J.E. Emburey	b Turner	1
M.W.W. Selvey	not out	38
R. Herkes	b East	1
A.A. Jones	c Pont, b East	1
	b 5, lb 2, w 1	8
		90

	O	M	R	W
Lever	6	1	23	—
Phillip	5	2	12	1
Turner	6	2	18	4
Pont	7	1	20	2
East	6	2	9	3

fall of wickets
1— 13, 2— 24, 3— 24, 4— 40, 5— 40, 6— 41, 7— 43, 8— 55, 9— 72

Umpires — W.E. Alley and R. Aspinall

Essex won by 99 runs
Middlesex won the toss and asked Essex to bat

v WORCESTERSHIRE AT WORCESTER
2 September

Worcestershire

G.M. Turner	c and b Turner	14
J.A. Ormrod	c and b Turner	22
Younis Ahmed	not out	90
E.J.O. Hemsley	b Pont	41
P.A. Neale	st Smith, b Pont	0
D.N. Patel	c Smith, b Pont	7
*D.J. Humphries	c East, b Lever	9
J.D. Inchmore	not out	6

†N. Clifford, J. Cumbes and P. Pridgeon did not bat

	b 1, lb 5, nb 4	10
	for 6 wkts	199

	O	M	R	W
Lever	8	1	40	1
Phillip	7	1	37	—
Turner	8	1	30	2
Pont	8	1	24	3
East	8	1	58	—

fall of wickets
1— 33, 2— 46, 3— 142, 4— 142, 5— 162, 6— 187

Essex

M.H. Denness	b Cumbes	39
A.W. Lilley	b Cumbes	31
K.S. McEwan	c Hemsley, b Cumbes	18
K.R. Pont	c Turner, b Patel	34
K.W.R. Fletcher	b Inchmore	37
B.R. Hardie	b Patel	5
S. Turner	not out	9
N. Phillip	run out	3
N. Smith	c Humphries, b Inchmore	6
R.E. East	run out	0
J.K. Lever	not out	4

	lb 7, w 4, nb 3	14
	for 9 wkts	200

	O	M	R	W
Inchmore	7	—	33	2
Pridgeon	8	1	27	—
Gifford	8	—	32	—
Cumbes	8	—	46	3
Patel	8	—	48	2

fall of wickets
1— 56, 2— 93, 3— 102, 4— 159, 5— 176, 6— 176, 7— 183, 8— 189, 9— 190

Umpires — P. Stevens and J.G. Langridge

Essex won by 1 wicket
Essex won the toss and asked Worcester to bat

v GLAMORGAN AT CHELMSFORD
9 September

Glamorgan

†A. Jones	not out	86
A.L. Jones	b East	39
R.C. Ontong	c and b Turner	1
P.D. Swart	c Lever, b Turner	10
J.A. Hopkins	c East, b Lever	29
M.A. Nash	not out	4

*E.W. Nash, D.A. Francis, A.E. Cordle, A.H. Wilkins and G.C. Holmes did not bat

	b 4, lb 15, w 2, nb 4	25
	for 4 wkts	194

	O	M	R	W
Lever	7	1	21	1
Phillip	7	1	33	—
Turner	8	1	35	2
Pont	8	—	50	—
East	8	—	30	1

fall of wickets
1—84, 2— 100, 3— 121, 4— 185

Essex

G.A. Gooch	c and b Cordle	22
A.W. Lilley	c E.W. Jones, b Swart	21
K.S. MacEwan	b Wilkins	6
K.R. Pont	run out	52
S. Turner	b Swart	4
K.W.R. Fletcher	b Swart	1
B.R. Hardie	b Swart	9
N. Phillip	c E.W. Jones, b Ontong	11
N. Smith	c Holmes, b Cordle	32
R.E. East	b Wilkins	4
J.K. Lever	not out	3
	b 1, lb 10, w 3, nb 1	15
		180

	O	M	R	W
Nash	8	1	37	—
Cordle	5.5	1	15	2
Wilkins	7	2	30	2
Swart	8	—	35	4
Ontong	8	1	48	1

fall of wickets
1— 37, 2— 46, 3— 54, 4— 77, 5— 83, 6— 104, 7— 134, 8— 147, 9— 160

Umpires — D.O. Oslear and C.T. Spencer

Glamorgan won by 14 runs
Glamorgan won the toss

Essex in the John Player League, 1979

Played 15; won 8; lost 6; no result 1; abandoned 1.
Position in League Table: sixth.

BATTING AVERAGES

Cap		Matches	Inns	NO	Runs	HS	Av	100s	50s	0s
1975	G.A. Gooch	11	11	2	303	77	33.66	—	2	1
1963	K.W.R. Fletcher	15	13	3	314	51*	31.40	—	1	1
1977	M.H. Denness	4	4	0	107	44	26.75	—	—	—
1974	B.R. Hardie	15	12	1	285	55*	25.90	—	1	—
1976	K.R. Pont	15	12	1	265	52	24.09	—	1	1
1970	S. Turner	15	11	3	146	20	18.25	—	—	—
1974	K.S. McEwan	15	15	2	237	45	18.23	—	—	—
1975	N. Smith	15	9	4	86	32	17.20	—	—	1
—	A.W. Lilley	15	15	1	219	31	15.64	—	—	—
1978	N. Phillip	14	10	2	60	15*	7.50	—	—	1
1970	J.K. Lever	15	7	3	16	5	4.00	—	—	1
1967	R.E. East	10	6	1	14	10*	2.80	—	—	4
1970	D.L. Acfield	6	2	2	4	3*	—	—	—	—
	Runs				2056					
	Byes				23					
	Leg Byes				79					
	Wides				35					
	No balls				20					
	TOTALS	15	127	25	2213	77	21.69	—	5	10

Mode of Dismissal

	Bowled	C & B	Caught	Ct WK	St	Lbw	Run Out	Total
Gooch	2	1	3	2	—	1	—	9
Fletcher	4	—	3	—	2	1	—	10
Denness	1	—	2	—	—	1	—	4
Hardie	6	—	1	2	—	1	1	11
Pont	2	—	5	—	1	—	3	11
Turner	3	1	3	—	—	1	—	8
McEwan	5	1	5	1	—	1	—	13
Smith	3	—	1	1	—	—	—	5
Lilley	4	—	5	4	—	—	1	14
Phillip	3	—	1	3	—	—	1	8
Lever	1	—	—	2	—	—	1	4
East	4	—	—	—	—	—	1	5
Totals	38	3	29	15	3	6	8	102

Scoring Rate
Runs scored from 3106 balls at a rate of 71.25 per 100 balls or 4.275 per over.

Striking Rate
Opponents took wickets at a rate of 30.45 balls per wicket.

BOWLING AVERAGES

	Type	M	I	O	Mdns	R	W	Av	4wI	Best
K.W.R. Fletcher	LB	15	2	0.5	0	5	1	5.00	—	1—4
R.E. East	SL	10	8	62	10	218	17	12.82	1	5—20
J.K. Lever	LFM	15	15	107.5	20	318	24	13.25	—	3—10
K.R. Pont	RM	15	15	106.3	14	428	21	20.38	1	4—24
N. Phillip	RFM	14	14	92.2	10	332	15	22.13	2	4—23
S. Turner	RFM	15	15	113	15	381	17	22.41	1	4—18
D.L. Acfield	OB	6	6	48	6	150	4	37.50	—	1—12
G.A. Gooch	RM	11	4	17	0	79	2	39.50	—	1—22
Runs						1911	101	18.92		
Byes						36				
Leg byes						112				
Wides						33				
No balls						21				
Run outs							3			
TOTALS		15	15	547.3	75	2113	104	20.31	5	5—20

Mode of Dismissal

	Bowled	C & B	Caught	Caught WK	St	Lbw	Total	Run Out
Fletcher	1	—	—	—	—	—	1	
East	6	—	6	2	2	1	17	
Lever	11	1	9	—	—	3	24	
Pont	8	1	7	1	2	2	21	
Phillip	5	—	7	—	—	3	15	
Turner	4	3	7	1	—	2	17	
Acfield	2	—	2	—	—	—	4	
Gooch	—	—	2	—	—	—	2	
Totals	37	5	40	4	4	11	101	3

Scoring Rate

Opponents scored their runs from 3285 balls at a rate of 64.32 per 100 balls or 3.859 per over.

Striking Rate

Wickets were taken at a rate of 31.59 balls per wicket.

CATCHES AND STUMPINGS

	N. Smith	4 catches	4 stumpings		
S. Turner	9 catches		G.A. Gooch	4 catches	
K.S. McEwan	7		J.K. Lever	3	
R.E. East	6		A.W. Lilley	3	
B.R. Hardie	6		D.L. Acfield	2	
K.R. Pont	5				

HIGHEST TOTAL

For: 200—9 in 39 overs v Worcestershire at Worcester

Against: 199—6 in 39 overs v Worcestershire at Worcester

LOWEST TOTAL

120—9 in 40 overs v Somerset at Bath

88 v Surrey at The Oval

CENTURY PARTNERSHIPS BY OPPONENTS (3)

135	2nd wkt	C.G. Greenidge & D.R. Turner	for Hampshire at Southampton
109	1st wkt	B.C. Rose & P.W. Denning	for Somerset at Bath
108	1st wkt	G.D. Mendis & P.J. Graves	for Sussex at Southend

FIFTIES

| For | 5 | Against | 8 |

SIXES (18)

K.R. Pont 9; G.A. Gooch 3; K.S. McEwan 2; K.W.R. Fletcher, A.W. Lilley, N. Phillip and S. Turner 1 each.

FOUR OR MORE WICKETS IN AN INNINGS (5)

N. Phillip (2)	4 for 23	v	Kent at Chelmsford
	4 for 26	v	Surrey at The Oval
R.E. East (1)	5 for 20	v	Yorkshire at Castle Park, Colchester
S. Turner (1)	4 for 18	v	Middlesex at Chelmsford
K.R. Pont (1)	4 for 24	v	Derbyshire at Chelmsford

FOUR OR MORE WICKETS IN AN INNINGS BY OPPONENTS (3)

D.J. Brown	5 for 22	for Warwickshire at Edgbaston, Birmingham
W. Hogg	4 for 23	for Lancashire at Ilford
P.D. Swart	4 for 35	for Glamorgan at Chelmsford

CAREER FIGURES — JOHN PLAYER LEAGUE MATCHES FOR ESSEX

Batting

	Matches	Inns	NO	Runs	HS	Av	100s	50s	0s	6s
D.L. Acfield (1970—79)	79	35	23	55	8	5.58	—	—	5	—
M.H. Denness (1977—79)	31	29	1	546	102	19.50	1	1	1	4
R.E. East (1969—79)	139	86	27	591	25*	10.01	—	—	9	3
K.W.R. Fletcher (1969—79)	143	135	14	3759	99*	31.06	—	27	6	18
G.A. Gooch (1973—79)	83	81	7	1740	90*	23.51	—	11	5	25
B.R. Hardie (1973—79)	83	76	4	1602	94	22.25	—	5	2	4
J.K. Lever (1969—79)	161	78	50	259	23	9.25	—	—	6	2
A.W. Lilley (1978—79)	17	17	1	286	54	17.87	—	1	—	1
M.S.A. McEvoy (1978)	1	1	0	7	7	7.00	—	—	—	—
K.S. McEwan (1974—79)	90	89	8	2196	123	27.11	2	11	5	25
N. Phillip (1978—79)	27	20	4	147	17*	9.18	—	—	1	2
K.R. Pont (1972—79)	108	94	16	1338	52	17.15	—	2	5	40
D.R. Pringle (1978)	2	1	1	8	8*	—	—	—	—	—
G.J. Saville (1970—73)	35	29	7	328	35	14.90	—	—	1	—
N. Smith (1974—79)	85	57	17	408	32	10.20	—	—	5	7
B. Taylor (1969—73)	78	77	3	1540	100	20.81	1	3	7	22
S. Turner (1969—79)	167	148	22	2375	87	18.84	—	8	8	28

Career Figures (where different from Essex figures)

	Matches	Inns	NO	Runs	HS	Av	100s	50s	0s	6s
M.H. Denness (1969—79)	133	125	16	3104	118*	28.47	4	14	10	
N. Smith (1970—79)	91	58	18	408	32	10.20	—	—	5	

Bowling and Fielding

	Overs	Mdns	Runs	Wkts	Av	4wI	Best	Runs p over	Balls p wkt	Ct	St
D.L. Acfield	555	55	2158	93	23.20	4	5—14	3.89	35.81	15	—
M.H. Denness	—	—	—	—	—	—	—	—	—	9	—
R.E. East	821.1	88	3300	138	23.91	4	6—18	4.02	35.70	64	—
K.W.R. Fletcher	1.5	0	11	1	11.00	—	1—4	6.01	11.00	52	—
G.A. Gooch	170	14	725	31	23.38	—	3—14	4.26	32.90	28	—
B.R. Hardie	—	—	—	—	—	—	—	—	—	28	—
J.K. Lever	1137.4	138	3801	228	16.67	8	5—13	3.34	29.94	35	—
A.W. Lilley	—	—	—	—	—	—	—	—	—	3	—
M.S.A. McEvoy	—	—	—	—	—	—	—	—	—	—	—
K.S. McEwan	—	—	—	—	—	—	—	—	—	29	—
N. Phillip	192.2	17	705	29	24.31	2	4—23	3.67	39.79	3	—
K.R. Pont	377.2	28	1704	63	27.04	1	4—24	4.52	35.94	24	—
D.R. Pringle	6	0	32	2	16.00	—	2—32	5.33	18.00	1	—
G.J. Saville	—	—	—	—	—	—	—	—	—	14	—
N. Smith	—	—	—	—	—	—	—	—	—	67	13
B. Taylor	—	—	—	—	—	—	—	—	—	62	19
S. Turner	1189.3	129	4566	225	20.29	8	5—35	3.84	31.72	63	—

Career Figures (where different from Essex figures)

M.H. Denness	—	—	—	—	—	—	—	—	—	63	—
N. Smith	—	—	—	—	—	—	—	—	—	69	13

CAREER BEST PERFORMANCES 1979

K.W.R. Fletcher	Best bowling: 1—4 v Leicestershire at Leicester
N. Phillip	Best bowling: 4—23 v Kent at Chelmsford
K.R. Pont	Highest score: 52 v Glamorgan at Chelmsford
	Best bowling: 4—24 v Derbyshire at Chelmsford
N. Smith	Highest score: 32 v Glamorgan at Chelmsford

The following batsmen had their most successful season:

A.W. Lilley	219 runs
K.R. Pont	265 runs (av 24.09)

The following bowlers had their most successful season:

N. Phillip	15 wickets (av 22.13)
K.R. Pont	21 wickets (av 20.38)

Gillette Cup

v LANCASHIRE AT OLD TRAFFORD
27 June

Lancashire

B. Wood	retired hurt	12
D. Lloyd	c Fletcher, b Pont	36
F.C. Hayes	c Hardie, b Pont	23
C.H. Lloyd	run out	76
J. Abrahams	c and b East	3
B.W. Reidy	b Turner	8
J. Simmons	not out	54
D.P. Hughes	not out	17
J. Lyon, W. Hogg and P.G. Lee did not bat		
	b 4, lb 12, w 1, nb 1	18
	for 5 wkts	247

	O	M	R	W
Lever	12	1	51	—
Phillip	12	1	70	—
Pont	12	3	25	2
Turner	12	—	44	1
East	12	1	39	1

fall of wickets
1— 73, 2— 82, 3— 89, 4— 120, 5— 209

Essex

M.H. Denness	st Lyon, b Hughes	27
G.A. Gooch	c and b Hughes	33
K.S. McEwan	c and b Simmons	12
K.W.R. Fletcher	run out	31
B.R. Hardie	b Hughes	2
R.E. East	b D. Lloyd	1
K.R. Pont	lbw, b Hogg	27
N. Phillip	b Lee	4
S. Turner	b Lee	18
N. Smith	b Hogg	6
J.K. Lever	not out	2
	b 2, lb 9, w 1, nb 2	14
		177

	O	M	R	W
Hogg	10	2	40	2
Lee	7.4	—	33	2
Hughes	12	3	22	3
Simmons	12	3	27	1
D. Lloyd	12	1	41	1

fall of wickets
1— 52, 2— 71, 3— 73, 4— 80, 5— 87, 6— 132, 7— 143, 8— 150, 9— 173

Umpires — C.T. Spencer and W.E. Phillipson

Lancashire won by 70 runs
Lancashire won the toss

CAREER BATTING AVERAGES FOR ESSEX

	Matches	Inns	NO	Runs	HS	Av	100s	50s	0s
D.L. Acfield (1970—77)	7	6	6	3	2*	—	—	—	—
M.H. Denness (1977—79)	5	4	0	105	71	26.25	—	1	—
R.E. East (1966—79)	22	15	3	124	38*	10.33	—	—	—
K.W.R. Fletcher (1963—79)	28	27	2	666	74	26.64	—	3	1
G.A. Gooch (1973—79)	12	11	0	217	61	19.72	—	1	1
B.R. Hardie (1973—79)	11	11	0	299	83	27.18	—	1	—
J.K. Lever (1968—79)	22	16	9	48	8	6.85	—	—	—
K.S. McEwan (1974—79)	10	10	1	305	63	33.88	—	2	1
N. Phillip (1978—79)	4	4	1	34	24*	11.33	—	—	—
K.R. Pont (1972—79)	12	11	1	126	39	12.60	—	—	—
D.R. Pringle (1978)	1	—	—	—	—	—	—	—	—
G.J. Saville (1964—72)	6	6	0	38	22	6.33	—	—	1
N. Smith (1974—79)	9	8	1	56	12	8.00	—	—	—
B. Taylor (1963—73)	19	17	0	221	31	13.00	—	—	—
S. Turner (1968—79)	22	18	2	331	50	20.68	—	1	1

Career Figures (where different from Essex figures)

	Matches	Inns	NO	Runs	HS	Av	100s	50s	0s
M.H. Denness (1963—79)	35	33	0	953	85	28.87	—	8	1
G.J. Saville (1964—72)	8	8	0	119	73	14.87	—	1	1
N. Smith (1970—79)	10	9	1	61	12	7.62	—	—	—

CAREER BOWLING AND FIELDING FOR ESSEX

	Overs	Mdns	Runs	Wkts	Av	4wI	Best	Runs p over	Balls p wkt	Ct	St
D.L. Acfield	69.3	9	256	4	64.00	—	2—51	3.68	104.25	3	—
M.H. Denness	—	—	—	—	—	—	—	—	—	1	—
R.E. East	203	40	521	15	34.73	1	4—28	2.57	81.20	7	—
K.W.R. Fletcher	6	1	16	1	16.00	—	1—16	2.67	36.00	14	—
G.A. Gooch	39	2	137	3	45.66	—	1—39	3.51	78.00	4	—
B.R. Hardie	—	—	—	—	—	—	—	—	—	3	—
J.K. Lever	233.4	49	631	40	15.77	5	5—8	2.70	35.05	3	—
K.S. McEwan	1	0	5	0	—	—	—	5.00	—	5	—
N. Phillip	39	2	202	6	33.66	—	2—35	5.18	39.00	—	—
K.R. Pont	58.4	8	200	9	22.22	—	2—18	3.41	39.11	2	—
D.R. Pringle	—	—	—	—	—	—	—	—	—	—	—
G.J. Saville	—	—	—	—	—	—	—	—	—	4	—
N. Smith	—	—	—	—	—	—	—	—	—	6	1
B. Taylor	—	—	—	—	—	—	—	—	—	20	3
S. Turner	200.5	44	574	29	19.79	—	3—16	2.86	41.55	5	—

Career Figures (where different from Essex figures)

	Overs	Mdns	Runs	Wkts	Av	4wI	Best	Runs p over	Balls p wkt	Ct	St
M.H. Denness	—	—	—	—	—	—	—	—	—	12	—
G.J. Saville	—	—	—	—	—	—	—	—	—	5	—

NEW RECORD WICKET PARTNERSHIPS

89	5th wkt	C.H. Lloyd & J. Simmons	for Lancashire at Old Trafford

Index